T0070094

Fishing Different

Techniques For Improving Success

Jake Bussolini

Edited by: C.H."Skip" Weber

authorHOUSE®

AuthorHouse™
1663 Liberty Drive
Bloomington, IN 47403
www.authorhouse.com
Phone: 1 (800) 839-8640

© *2016 Jake Bussolini. All rights reserved.*

No part of this book may be reproduced, stored in a retrieval system, or transmitted by any means without the written permission of the author.

Published by AuthorHouse 03/22/2016

ISBN: 978-1-5049-8671-7 (sc)
ISBN: 978-1-5049-8668-7 (e)

Library of Congress Control Number: 2016904699

Print information available on the last page.

Any people depicted in stock imagery provided by Thinkstock are models, and such images are being used for illustrative purposes only. Certain stock imagery © Thinkstock.

This book is printed on acid-free paper.

Because of the dynamic nature of the Internet, any web addresses or links contained in this book may have changed since publication and may no longer be valid. The views expressed in this work are solely those of the author and do not necessarily reflect the views of the publisher, and the publisher hereby disclaims any responsibility for them.

Contents

Introduction

Seventy years of fishing experience should, one would think, make me a very skilled angler. Among the many things I have learned over my lifetime is that we humans might have to go through changes in culture and habits several times along the way. I have tried to make it a personal objective to learn something new every day, and it seems that it is only in the last twenty years or so that things around me have changed so fast that I can now hardly keep up with them. Learning something new is now not a goal, but a requirement. At the upper middle age of 80, I think I have done fairly well adapting to the technological changes that have taken place around me. One thing I have learned is that when my smart phone has me confused with its updates or new features, I simply hand it to my 8-year old granddaughter to get it straightened out for me. Despite my formal education as an engineer, when my computer fails to react as I wish it too, I simply shut it down, wait 10 seconds and turn it back on. That corrects my problem most of the time. (Oh! Excuse me. I should try to use the correct terminology: re-boot the machine.)

When it comes to fishing, however, I find myself in a peculiar situation. It sometimes seems that nearly everything I learned during the first 60 years of my life seems no longer to be valid. Or at least that's what I am led to believe by all of the recent outdoor magazine articles I read. The last 20 years have presented me with so many new innovations and new techniques, each one being better than the last for catching fish. What is a person to do in this rapidly changing environment?

The approach that I have taken to uncover the truth about modern fishing is to carefully study the details of the science of fishing as it relates to the sport of fishing. During the last twenty years I have collected so much information from my studies that during that time I have published six books about fresh water fishing. My studies, of course, almost always involved actual fishing experiences in different lakes and rivers around the country. Each one of these fishing experiences has the dual purpose of enjoyment and research. As I have continually reminded my understanding wife, his is tough work, but someone has to do it so it might as well be me."

On most of my fishing trips over the last 20 years, I kept detailed records of my catches, weather conditions, and water conditions. Writing in my notebooks was so constant a habit it often irritated my fishing partners. The details in my records, however, provide excellent support for the development of my fishing theories.

Those who have read my books know that I have not always taken the conventional path to getting answers to puzzling questions. More often than not I have been successful in crushing age-old myths which have guided anglers for decades. Some of these new truths are so startling that "old timers" have difficulty accepting them and adopting their angling techniques to the "new normal." I must remind readers that at the age of 80, I too will soon be an "old timer."

When I study proposed new angling techniques, I can't help but reflect back to where and when it all started. They say a person should never forget his roots. Well, my fishing roots started in 1944 when I was eight years old. I was born and raised in the small New England town of Avon, Connecticut. This town was mostly populated by European immigrants who were skilled blue collar trades people. Like my Dad, who was a carpenter, the income level of most of the population put them in what we today call the middle class. But back then we didn't think in terms of classes, everyone just worked for a living and in most cases both husband and wife worked full time. Vegetable gardens dotted nearly every back yard. Nearly every family had at least one hunter or fisherman, not necessarily because they enjoyed the sport, but sometimes out of necessity for a food source. There were very few two-car families when I was growing up. It was a matter of affordability.

Avon was an interesting town as I look back on it, but back then we never seemed to think much about the history or heritage of our town. It was simply the place we lived. The town was incorporated in 1830 and the European heritage of most of the families fostered great patriotism among its citizens. During the Civil War, when Avon had a population of only 1059, 98 men went to serve in the army. Twenty five of those men died. During WWI, 77 men went to war and fortunately all of them returned – a very rare happening. In WWII, 300 of the town's men and women went to war with 13 never returning alive. Vivid in my memory was the town's honor role that stood in the town square containing all of the names of those who served and died in the wars. This was the place that the annual Memorial Day parade ended in honor of those men and women, and nearly every resident of the town attended this ceremony. During all of my years growing up in Avon, there was never a riot, never a demonstration, never a flag burning and to the best of my recollection never a murder or even a break-in. WOW! What a boring existence that must have been. I do remember the three party telephones, and strange as it may sound, I still remember our telephone party line number: it was 357 ring 3. Everyone owned one radio and the young boys like me would sit intently by the radio on Wednesday and Friday at 7:30 pm to listen to The Lone Ranger. I also remember when gasoline was priced at nineteen cents a gallon.

There were no real significant happenings in Avon, as I recall, that occupy a place in history. The town was bounded to the west by Talcott Mountain and at the top of that mountain was the Heublein Tower used as a summer place and social gathering spot for some of Hartford's elite. The owners, of course, were the owners of the Heublein Liquor Company. In 1950 the tower was used in conjunction with the opening ceremonies of Bradley Field, now named Bradley International Airport in Windsor Locks, Connecticut. It was during a party at the tower that the leaders of the National Republican Party asked General Dwight David Eisenhower to be the party's candidate for President of the United States.

Transportation during the early years of Avon was assisted by the Farmington Canal which ran between Avon and New Haven, Connecticut. The canal was opened in 1828 with mules towing barges loaded with cargo and passengers along its 38-mile length. This trip took 10 hours and cost each passenger $1.75.

But enough about the town's history that would seem to have no bearing on anyone's fishing skills. There were three industries in Avon that kept everyone employed; dairy farming, tobacco farming, and the Ensign-Bickford Company, which manufactured explosives for the military. The company literally owned the town for many years. To assist their manufacturing process, Ensign-Bickford needed steam, and to generate the steam they needed large quantities of water. To get the needed water they built a dam on a small stream and created a small lake which we all called Stub Pond. Why that name? I don't know and I have never been able to determine it through my research. BUT! Stub Pond is where it all started for me. A small local fishing club was formed and was given permission by Ensign-Bickford to stock the pond with trout.

My Dad and Mom build our first house about ½ half mile up the road from Stub Pond. Well, it was more than just a road – it was CT Route 44, the main artery from Hartford to Albany, New York. My Dad joined this small fishing club. The annual dues were $2 per year. At the ripe old age of 8, I didn't need a state fishing license and the fishing club had no children as members, so my Dad convinced the club that they should permit youngsters to fish in their pond and join the club for 50¢ a year. Of course I joined.

My Dad taught me how to make the ½-mile walk from home to the pond and after one lesson, I was on my own. I walked to Stub Pond every day after school and every Saturday. My Dad accompanied me on many Saturdays and I will always remember the basic fishing facts that he pounded into my head. First and foremost was to always respect the older members of the club because they paid a lot more than I did to fish. The second rule was to never make any noise. Fishing, he would say, requires silence. Noise of any kind will scare away the fish. I had one metal telescoping fishing rod and a reel that had no bearings or gears. I would sometimes use a small rock as a weight and a cork from a wine bottle as a bobber. My fishing line was a black braided line that seemed like its strength was about 100 pounds, but at that age I had no idea what line strength meant.

I always went to the pond with a soup can filled with worms, my rod and reel with no spare tackle, and no net. I had a few favorite spots where I found running water. I would pull up a rock or a log to sit on and cut two forked sticks, one to stick into the ground to prop up my fishing rod and the other to string up the fish that I caught because trout were never thrown back unless they were under the 6-inch legal size. I might move two or three times during a three hour fishing day and most of the time I would catch my limit of five trout.

One evening my Dad received a call from the President of the fishing club. Some of the members had complained that I was only paying 50¢ a year and I was catching nearly all of the fish in the pond. They were considering making a new rule that would require that I either limit the days that I fish or raise my club membership fee to $2. My Dad was a relatively quiet man but when he got mad he was hard to deal with. His response to the club President was that we would both quit the club and build a boat so we could fish in the nearby reservoirs. He put $2.50 into an envelope and mailed it to the fishing club with a note of resignation for both of us.

He was a man of his word because the next day he informed me that he had ordered a Chris Craft boat kit and we were going to build a boat together. Build a boat we did. It was a sixteen foot plywood boat and he purchased a used Chris Craft 10 Hp motor. We had no trolling motor and, of course, no sonar fish finder just the boat. He heard about a trolling plate that could be attached to the motor to slow the speed of the boat and, of course, he purchased one. Every Saturday we fished a local lake and sometimes a nearby reservoir. We would troll for trout.

My Dad was one of those people who were taught that you had to be ready to drop your line in the water at sunrise, or whatever time the local law permitted. When we launched our new boat, we always left the house one hour before sunrise to be on the water as early as possible. He believed, as many anglers do, that the period between sunrise and noon is the best time to catch fish. It actually took me more than 50 years to prove that theory incorrect.

When we launched the boat in the morning, we each had one set-up: a rod, reel and strong line. We trolled the lake with a rig that was called a Davis Spinner. This was a rig that we manufactured ourselves. It required three shiny spinner blades for flash, and piano wire for connecting structure. We would go to a local junk yard and pick out a couple of old headlamps from a wrecked car. These headlamps had a very shiny reflector inside and were made of hard steel which made them very hard to cut. We would cut three leaf type blades for each rig. Each reflecting blade was a different size with the largest one closest to the rod and the smallest one closest to the bait, which was normally a hook and night crawler. The three spinner blades were connected together with 6 inch pieces of piano wire. The entire rig was rather heavy but it worked very well for the lake trout. The shiny blades were highly polished chrome plated metal that provided plenty of flash for the rig. The flash, of course was only to attract the attention of the fish toward the night crawler that was attached to the single hook at the end of the rig. It took me several years to realize that the blades banging against the piano wire sent out a lot of noise, but no one ever thought of this noise as an attractor. Remember, quiet was the word in those days, noise scared the fish away, another myth that needed study.

This was my introduction to fishing for trout in ponds and lakes. My Dad and I fished for years using this technique and we caught more than our share of fish. How simple it was, no fishing box full of lures; no multiple rods and reels; no sonar fish finders; no trolling motors, I didn't even own a crank bait lure until after I finished college, or a reel that actually had gears and bearings for that matter.

What a different life it was back in the 40's and 50's. We didn't have quite as many things to worry about that could make us unhappy so most folks considered themselves happy people. Men married women and women married men. When a marriage took place the woman actually took on the last name of her husband except under very unusual circumstances. No one cared what type of flag or the size of the flag that you flew near your home because everyone understood that this was America and the American flag was the only one that counted. Road signs, billboards, and legal papers were always written in English because after all, that was the language of America. Nearly every citizen in my home town came to America from Europe and they became American citizens by adhering to the process that was in place to do so. I don't believe that there was a welfare program back then. Everyone worked and paid their taxes and didn't expect anyone else to pay their way. I don't believe that there was a psychologist or a psychiatrist within 50 miles of my home town. Schools taught the three R's and history and the churches and the families dealt with culture, morals, and sin.

Perhaps you might think at this point that talking about these social and cultural issues in a fishing book is a little out of place and perhaps it is, but the simplicity of life not too many years ago left plenty of time for family, and the family traditions that resulted, like hunting and fishing. Kids, both male and female, were taught about life from their parents and taught about right and wrong by their church regardless of their specific beliefs. What I learned about the outdoors from my dad seems like such simple theory. Fish lived in the water, they had to eat to survive, and they loved to eat earth worms. All an angler had to do was put a worm in front of a fish and it was game on. By today's standards, that was **Fishing Different.** From the perspective of the way we fish today, the old methods seem so crude and outdated but were they really?

Recent discoveries tell us that the fish hook dates back more than 42,000 years. WOW! That's before radio, television, George Washington or Abraham Lincoln and even far earlier than the telephone. But, the fish hook of that time used essentially the same concept as it does today. It was designed from bone or shells and its purpose was to get lodged in the throat of a fish. Today's fish hooks come in hundreds of varieties, sizes and shapes but their basic purpose is still to get stuck in a fish, permitting the angler to retrieve the fish from its normal habitat. So from the point of view of the fish hook, are we really **Fishing Different** today?

A good friend and fishing associate of mine uses the example of fishing in your bath tub. You can fish as long as you want there and use the most expensive equipment and lures, but you will never catch a fish because there are no fish in your bath tub. Finding the fish is as much of a challenge today as it was 100 years ago. I was successful catching trout in a small pond because I always fished where I knew there was moving water. I didn't understand why that produced more fish. It just did. Today the problem is the same. The angler needs to understand the waters that are being fished and determine the best locations for catching fish. The difference today is that we have hundreds of different types of equipment to aid us in finding fish. We are **Fishing Different** today because we have the advantage of decades of research and technology to assist us, perhaps maybe too much for the sake of protecting our waters and the fish that we depend on for continued good fishing.

This book takes a look at many of the techniques and technologies that are available to anglers today to assist them in catching more and bigger fish. We will discuss in detail some of the historical techniques and theories that may or may not be applicable today. The facts presented will crush several of the age old myths about our sport and perhaps even make it a little simpler to practice the sport. Since it has always been my habit to explain my theories by citing the science behind them, I will continue to do so here, and where possible, I will back new theories by data from tests and actual fishing experience. My idea of **Fishing Different** is to simplify the understanding of the technology, get rid of the garbage, and fish simply and successfully.

Chapter One

In The Beginning

"It is the mark of an educated mind to be able to entertain a thought without accepting it"

Aristotle

The history of fishing as we know it today can be traced to one of its earliest pieces of fishing tackle, called a gorge. It is questionable just how far back we have to search to find the origin of the gorge. I have a great deal of respect for the world's paleontologists because they dedicate their lives to searching for the tiny pieces of evidence, which when put together, form the basis for solidifying a new chapter of history or filling gaps in already discovered information. I must admit that I have never indulged my desire to read any of the books written by these scientists. I'm sure that the pure excitement of the contents of such a book would keep me on the edge of my seat, but instead I have depended on the interpretations of others who have read them to summarize the contents.

As a practical scientist, I enjoy making my own interpretations of the facts of history and my research on the gorge has permitted me to do that. My conclusions, of course, are supported by historical facts. I have taken the liberty of putting these facts into a logical and perhaps more interesting story. It was recently announced that scientists had discovered the remains of a primitive gorge – or fish hook – that has been dated back more than 42,000 years.

Picture the shores of Lake Turkana located in the Region of Olduvai in East Africa. A young Neanderthal named Gronk was searching the shores of this lake for food. The brains of the adult Neanderthals are believed to have been seriously under-developed, but the younger generations were beginning to develop a thought process to better understand the world around them.

Gronk observed large birds swooping down close to the lake's shoreline to pick up what looked like small rocks. The birds grabbed the rocks, flew to a higher altitude and dropped the rocks to hit large boulders below. They then descended to where the rocks had landed and proceeded to start a process which looked very much like they were eating.

At first Gronk was amused by this process and showed his excitement by jumping up and down each time the birds landed to start their feeding process. Eventually the excitement gave way to curiosity and Gronk ran to pick up one of the dropped rocks before the bird could retrieve it. He noticed that it was not a rock at all but some form of sea life. Dropping the item to the rocks below cracked the shell, revealing something inside that looked to be eatable.

Gronk took this strange object back to his family dwelling and after a short gathering, the elders decided that this was an excellent source of food. In those ancient times any event that was unusual or previously unknown, was believed to be a signal from one of the many Gods they worshiped. Excited by this latest gift, the entire colony rushed to the shores of the lake to search for more of these odd creatures. The group was so excited about the ease with which they could gather food that they began the process of breaking the creatures open by crushing them on the shoreline rocks and eating the food on the spot instead of taking it back to their dwelling place. Over a period of time the shores of Lake Turkana became littered with the broken shells. The shells were so abundant that Gronk's family got sloppy and often left some portion of the food attached to the cracked and crushed shells. Normal winds and weather would often wash these remains into the water.

Some months later Gronk was again walking the shores of Lake Turkana when he came across the wiggling body of a large fish that had been washed ashore. Gronk grabbed the fish in amazement that such a fine meal simply came on shore to him. Again, his belief was that it was a gift from the Gods. Gronk's community was familiar with this type of fish. They would often wade into the shallow water to catch the smaller fish by hand as a source of food. They had, however, never seen or caught one of this size.

Gronk was suddenly overcome with the same curiosity he felt when he first saw the birds dropping the shells to the rocks below. In his simple way he wondered what had caused this big fish to be washed ashore, still alive but struggling for life. As he began to prepare the big fish to present it as a fine meal to his family, Gronk noticed that there was a sharp shell from one of the discarded shells lodged across the throat of the big fish. The fish had apparently picked up one of the half-eaten and discarded shells to pick out the food remaining inside. The aggressiveness of the fish caused it to swallow the entire shell with its jagged edges which then became lodged in its throat. The fish was now unable to process its needed oxygen through its gills and started to die.

We will never know just how long it took for the Neanderthals to figure out what they had discovered, but more than 42,000 years later, many of these gorges were uncovered with evidence that somewhere in history someone figured out that if they tied a vine or thread to the gorge, it could be baited with some eatable material and used to catch large quantities of the big fish.

Most of what we know about that period in human development tells us that the simplicity of the Neanderthal mind did not permit them to do much reasoning on things as complicated as the discovery of the gorge. What they could not understand they simply looked to the stars and attributed new and amazing discoveries as gifts sent down to them by their Gods.

Paleontologists researching this area found thousands of bones from large fish in areas where the Neanderthal communities were living and along with the fish bones were several crudely carved shells, made into the shape of hooks (or gorges) which would get lodged in the throats of the big fish. The vines that were attached to the crude hooks permitted the angler to retrieve the fish much like we do today.

How long did it take to progress from that first fish brought to the camp by Gronk, to the point where fish were regularly being caught by attaching a vine – or other stringed material – which made fishing as we know it today a regular method of acquiring food? Did it take ten years or ten thousand years? We don't really know except we can conclude that it took a long time compared to today's technology development speed.

There have been two or three significant theories put forth over hundreds of years of history concerning the creation, growth, and development of the human species. I suspect that during the next several hundred years, these conflicting theories will continue to be debated. As I mentioned earlier we have seen enormous and almost unimaginable technological advances over the last fifty years, including the harnessing of American ingenuity to set foot on another terrestrial body, the moon. I suspect that in the next ten years we will set foot on Mars or some other nearby world. What tremendous strides mankind has made to achieve such advances. Can we even imagine what progress mankind will make during the next hundred years?

But let's step back a bit. 42,000 years after the first fish was caught using a gorge and vine, we are still catching fish using a baited hook and line. Not much has changed over this vast period of time. Why? We now use metal to make our hooks. Vines have been replaced with a variety of different synthetic materials, and we have invented hundreds of thousands of different types of baits to attract the fish. BUT, to catch a fish we still depend on getting a gorge stuck in the mouth of a fish, permitting us to retrieve it for food or entertainment.

Why has there been no demand to harness the ingenuity of man to challenge the basic theories that have guided our fishing habits for years? No need say I. The one thing that has remained constant over the years is the prize – the fish. New species may have been discovered and new techniques developed to add flavor to a fine meal, but a fish is still a fish. Its purpose in life has never changed. Nature has provided fish the instinct for survival. From birth, a fish dedicates its life to eating and taking steps necessary to prevent being eaten by larger predators. The greater natural goal of every species of fish is to procreate itself so that the specie continues to thrive. That's it! There is nothing more complicated surrounding the life of a fish. In its simplest form, fishing is simply about putting food in front of a fish that has no other thought in its mind but eating. Let's not be naive, it is not as simple as that, but it's also not as complicated as some would make us believe.

My studies have convinced me that I can reduce some very cumbersome theories to the simplest concepts. I am convinced that most anglers seriously over-complicate the practice of catching fish to their detriment. A focus on the right elements will improve success substantially. I will discuss these elements in greater detail later in this book.

There are three things that directly affect fish behavior: the condition of the water in which they live; the availability of a food source; and the position and penetration of the sun on the water. All other factors that have been advertised as important are effects and not causes of behavioral changes.

As a relatively healthy and mentally developed man, it seems quite obvious to me. If we understand the various aspects of this premise we will have a better grasp of how to improve our fishing skills. I cannot help but wonder, however, how many years or perhaps decades (or even centuries) it took the less mentally developed Neanderthal minds to get from that crude cracked shell to a well designed hook mechanism with a vine attached. When and how did those simple minded humanoids figure out where the best places were to catch the fish? And how did their ability to catch fish change with the seasons or the weather?

For the most part the environment in which a fish lives has not changed significantly over the millennia. There are species that thrive in the salt waters of the oceans, and different species that thrive in fresh water. The presence of dissolved oxygen in the water permits the fish to absorb the oxygen needed to sustain life, just as we humans get our oxygen from the air we breathe. The similarities in the basic necessities of life are so common between man and all species of fish, that my theories about catching fish are often based on thinking about how I would perform under the same conditions that the fish has been placed in. If it's hot, I want to cool off. If it's cold I want a warmer environment. If I'm threatened I want to hide or defend myself. When I am hungry, I want to eat. Fish have all of the same reactions: the difference is simply the environment in which they are permitted to react. To become a better angler and catch bigger and better fish I believe we must always maintain an understanding of the few basics that I have mentioned. However, there is one very important difference between humans and fish. The brain of a typical fresh water fish is about the size of a human fingernail if it were compared to a human brain. Because of this reduced size, there are important human brain functions which are missing in fish. Fish have no central cortex in their brain as humans do. It is this central cortex that permits us to think and reason and place things in our memory. Fish have no such capability so they can't remember, think, or reason. Every action of a fish is based on natural instinct rather than logic or reasoning. This is somewhat similar to the way Neanderthals reacted to things they did not understand. They simply considered them an Act Of God. For now my most important point is that as anglers we must understand the basic needs of all fish and direct our fishing techniques to satisfying those needs, successfully improving our fishing results.

One thing we have learned over the years is that as soon as we become satisfied we have solved a problem, something will change that will alter our conclusion. Can we conclude that once Gronk and his community discovered that fish could be caught for food using clams and oysters as bait, that the source of fish was never-ending? Or can we assume that as Gronk's community continued to pick up their new shellfish food source that eventually this source became depleted, perhaps also depleting the shellfish as a food for the fish, driving the fish to another area to feed. Even the simplest Neanderthal mind could reason that when the fish disappeared due to the lack of food, they (the community) would have to change their fishing location to a place where the food source for the fish was abundant.

The reason I stated my uncertainty about the time span for the learning process of the Neanderthals is that documents reveal that their brain development was very slow. Their development started with a minimal ability to reason. Their thought process was not complicated by any events that surrounded them. Most of the younger generation did not learn from their elders, except perhaps for items dealing with basic survival. As the new generations developed, they appeared to have a greater ability to reason and think. In other words, their brains were developing into what we witness today as the ability of modern humans.

Most of us (middle ages and above) developed our basic habits from the experiences of our parents. Our first automobile was probably the same brand driven by our parents. We probably voted for the same political party as our parents until we got interested enough in politics to think for ourselves. Work ethics, religious leanings and cultural basics were all based on what we were taught by our parents. This transitional process was nearly a reverse of the Neanderthals where reasoning and basic intelligence was the result of growth of the younger generations.

Is it possible that we are seeing another reversal of that cultural development process today? Technology in some areas has moved so fast that the youngsters seem more capable of adopting it than their parents. The logic and reasoning that the older generations developed seems to be giving way to less thinking and more "Googling" for answers. Many of the studies and findings that we took as gospel, we are now finding were in error.

A recent Associated Press report indicated that a group of current scientists conducted a study of more than 100 past experiments in the area of psychology treatments. The results of these past experiments and tests were used to develop treatments for patients for many years. Carefully controlled re-tests of the results of past experiments showed that 60% of those experiments produced results that were incorrect by current medical standards. Does this mean that past scientific tests were incorrectly recorded or reported?

Certainly not, but this is a clear indication that over the course of time things progress and knowledge changes.

I have found the same results when examining some of the fishing practices that have been handed down from past generations which have become standard throughout the angling community. Many of these practices were based on data and testing that, by today's standards, are no longer valid. That is why I have done extensive recording of my fishing experiences and in some cases run extensive tests to validate my conclusions. Throughout this book I will discuss these differences in opinion. As readers, you might find some of my findings and conclusions shocking because they destroy the foundation of your beliefs and fishing habits. You may choose to ignore my findings and continue to fish the old ways, but I feel confident that if you approach my suggestions with an open mind, you may start **Fishing Different.**

CHAPTER TWO

Back to Basics Permits Breaking Through the Bubble of Failure

"Success is the ability to go from failure to failure without losing your enthusiasm"

Sir Winston Churchill

During the period when I was writing this book, one of the world's greatest golfers was suddenly struggling to maintain credibility and his professional standing throughout the golf world. Tiger Woods has for years amazed golf fans and his competitors by winning many of golf's most prestigious victories. Suddenly due to personal setbacks and injuries, his performance deteriorated to the point where he was no longer even considered a serious contender.

During my lifetime of following different professional sports, I have seen this dilemma repeated many times. Some of the effected individuals worked tirelessly to overcome their defects while others seemed never to recover to their

14

original levels of excellence. I have noticed, however, that those who succeeded in shedding their demons to return to stardom have one small thing in common they buried their pride and went back to the most basic elements of their game. Somewhere in this process they found some small flaw that they had overlooked and when that flaw was corrected they once again rose to the top of their game.

Because of my modest success as a fishing writer, I have been given the opportunity to participate in events like lectures, book signings and other appearance where I get a chance to discuss fishing with large and diverse groups of people. On nearly every occasion I sense the same level of passion among my audiences, they all want to learn how to catch greater quantities of fish and also to increase the quality of the fish that they catch.

It is very common to find that the average angler today has been overly influenced by the marketing elements of the sport. They buy the newest and latest equipment and often fall victim to the enormous technology advances that have been made with accessories to the sport, especially with electronics. I have concluded over the years that many if not most of these new and advanced aids to the sport have become more of a distraction than an aid to the average angler. While attempting to learn the ins and outs of the new equipment, many anglers are taking their eye "off the ball" about the very basic elements of the sport of fishing.

I'm going to try real hard in this book, not to sound too disparaging about all of these electronic aids to the sport. I have tried most of the new equipment and still have a good deal of it mounted on my boats. I feel however, that with the exception of the electronic fish finder, I have been rather successful using this equipment as a supplement to my basic fishing knowledge and not as my primary tool for catching fish.

It might be worth telling a short personal story here to illustrate my point. Nearly 40 years ago I was a relatively young engineer, struggling for recognition in a large Aerospace Company. I was surrounded by airplanes and airplane related equipment every minute of the day while I was on the job. As an electrical engineer, I felt somewhat intimidated by this constant airplane dialog so I decided to join the company's flying club to learn how to fly.

I passed all of the preliminary hurdles and tests and eventually took and passed the test for my Private Pilot's license. Feeling that there was more that I could learn to be a smarter and safer pilot, I took advanced courses for higher pilot ratings. Shortly after receiving my instrument rating, I purchased an airplane from the flying club. The club had an instrument rated Cessna 172 that was close to needing an engine overhaul and they decided to sell the airplane rather than spend the money for a new engine.

The airplane contained all of the equipment needed for instrument flight, but it was all very basic equipment. What this meant was that the pilot became a very important part of the system of instruments. The dials and gauges would provide all of the information needed for safe flight, but the pilot was needed as the processing computer to make it all play together. This suited my objective just fine.

As for the engine, I was concerned. Every minute that I was in that aircraft I would be placing my life in the hands of that engine, a mechanism that I knew very little about. I contacted an acquaintance of mine who was a licensed engine mechanic. I informed him that I wanted to perform the overhaul of the engine myself if possible to better understand the basics of engine technology. He informed me that current FAA regulations would not permit me to do the entire overhaul, but working with him through the process, I could do much of the work except for a few actions that needed to be performed by him. During the course of that engine overhaul, I became very familiar with every part of that engine and felt that I had a good understanding of the basics of operation.

I owned and flew that aircraft for more than 30 years, making a few equipment replacements and upgrades to keep the equipment current with existing regulations. At each stage of these upgrades, there was always new and more modern equipment available that was advertized to lighten the pilot work load. I always went with upgrades that met the minimum requirements and kept the pilot in total control.

At the ripe young age of 75, I attended a one day program sponsored by the FAA called the WINGS program. This program is designed to keep pilots current with existing changes and those being planned. There were approximately twenty pilots in attendance at this program which was held in Hickory North Carolina. Needless to say, every other attendee was significantly younger than me. For eight hours I listened to dialog about all of the new things that were coming. Pilots were using their Ipads and even their cell phones as routing navigation equipment. We were informed that the FAA had plans to completely change the entire navigation system around the world, abandoning the VHF Omni-directional Radio system (VOR) that had been used for worldwide navigation for decades, in favor of a modified GPS system. This change would require that nearly every small aircraft owner would have to spend a great deal on money upgrading to the new system requirements. The excitement in the audience was noticeable and seemed to focus on the fact that the pilot would have all of this new equipment to play with which would make the navigation job simpler. They talked of I pads strapped to the instrument panel and cell phones and other communication equipment mounted in other areas of the instrument panel.

I tolerated this dialog as long as I could and finally I raised my hand and when recognized I faced the audience and asked "Most of you here today fly as single pilots as I do. We have no co pilot to assist us. While you are busy playing with all of you new equipment, watching your new map display GPS equipment and working all of the touch screen equipment, who the hell is flying the plane?" Everyone in that room was experienced enough to know that a distracted pilot who lets his attention be diverted for a mere moment, can get his aircraft into a seriously dangerous situation which often creates a life or death condition.

The room went silent for a few moments and I could feel the emotions of most of the audience thinking, "who is this old guy with his old ideas?" That was the moment that I decided to quit flying, the moment that I knew it was time to sell my aircraft and give up a hobby that I loved so dearly. It was obvious to me that the future of private aviation was about to get less dependent on experienced pilots and more dependent upon electronic accessories to ease the pilot workload.

On my short flight home that day, I kept recalling the many times that as an integrated part of my aircraft system, I was required to make instant calculations in my head of wind speed changes that would affect my fuel consumption. I thought of the many times that I had requested a route change because I determined from experience that there were delays ahead. These were things I did as a pilot because I was part of the basic airplane system, I always reverted back to basics which required that I, as the pilot, made the decisions that would keep me and my passengers safe. I was not willing to relinquish that responsibility, so I retired from flying and sold my airplane.

Don't get me wrong, I am a strong supporter of moving our society ahead and I am proud of the technological progress that our country and other modernized nations have made that have improved out lifestyle and influenced our economy. I sometimes fear however, that all of the new and apparently revolutionary changes are coming at us so fast that we tend to lose site of the basic principles that made us a great nation.

Shifting this philosophical approach to focus on the subject at hand, fishing, there are many similarities that sometimes lead me to believe that we are forgetting the basics of our sport. I recently talked with the manager of a relatively large sporting goods store who told me that his fishing related departments had more than 200,000 different pricing SKU's. This means that the store stocked more than 200,000 different items related to fishing. He indicated that fishing lures accounted for more than 30,000 SKU's. I walked the isles of this store and counted more than 50 different packages of fishing hooks, 30 different packages of lead weights and 20 different bobber arrangements. In the fresh water section alone, there were more than 200 different rod and reel combinations on display and the reel display housed nearly 100 different individual reels priced from $29.95 up to over $500.

During my monthly lectures on various fishing subjects, I often take recorded notes of the questions that I am asked, and I get a fair amount of feedback from those who read my books. When I take all of this information and try to digest it in order to determine how I can best help people improve their fishing experiences, I quickly come to one conclusion, sticking to basics is the best help that I can give to those looking to improve their fishing results. Nearly everyone wants to improve their catch rate but most people keep doing the same things wrong time and time again. I can only conclude that anglers are always willing to try what someone else has recommended, but they rarely take the time to truly understand why things happen the way they do.

Lets lock in our minds a couple of fishing basics that never change and likely never will. The habits of fish have not changed since the beginning of recorded history. Fish eat whatever is most dominant in their specific environment. Most fish want to eat living things and these are the insects, bugs, worms and other small living things that either reside in the same waters or are washed into those waters by the rain and winds. Most species of fish have a couple periods during the day that they prefer to eat and these periods often change from day to day. Regardless of these normal feeding periods nearly every fish will be attracted to food at any time during the day or night that they see it. In other words a fish will rarely pass up a meal if it is put in front of it. Lastly and perhaps most important, natures instincts tell fish that living things have the greatest amount of protein which is the essential element of their growth. Things like earth worms, bugs and other small fish provide the highest levels of protein and they have been the favorite food of fish since the beginning of time. Despite the tremendous growth in the use of artificial baits, the common earth worm or night crawler is still the number one food desired by all species of fish.

Let's think about that fact for a moment because it is a good example of how, with a little logic and reasoning, we can improve our catch rate. The waters of our lakes and rivers are not the normal habitat for earth worms, they live in the dirt under the surface of solid ground. Think back to the many times you have walked along a roadway, sidewalk or parking lot after a heavy rain. The pavement is covered with small earth worms that came to the surface to get the fresh rain water. Continued heavy rains will wash these worms into storm drains and culverts that eventually drain into the ponds, lakes and rivers. After thousands of years of survival and existence, don't you think that the fish, through pure repetition and habit, also know that these rains wash the worms into the waters? Again, this is another of nature's instinctive teachings.

As humans with all of our powers of reasoning, what can we learn from this? Search for the areas of your fishing grounds where small rain streams, culverts and drain pipes flow into the waters. These areas are crowded with worms and they will also be crowded with game fish. Fresh water flowing into a water body will also usually create new green growth along the shoreline so anywhere you see fresh growth at the shore, there is a good chance that at some point water is flowing and bringing this precious food to the fish.

I can provide one tip that I have learned about the above situation. The area where drain water normally flows into a lake or river is often very shallow water and most fish do not like to spend a great deal of time in the shallow water. They will come in to gather food and then move to a deeper area. Find the area closest to the in-flow where the bottom drops off and the water get deeper. Fish this area to improve your success.

This is a good time for another tip. If you are fishing an area and you get no action at all for a period of 20 minutes, move to another area, don't be the victim of the "bathtub syndrome". There is a back side to this rule. Never leave biting fish. If there is one fish in the area that is hungry, there is a good chance that there are more fish nearby. If the fish are biting, continue to fish that area until the bite stops for 20 minutes then try another area.

As Sir Winston Churchill said, people are repeating failure time after time but they are successful people because they approach each failure effort with great enthusiasm. This statement is applicable to the subject at hand but unfortunately I disagree with the premise because I hate to lose. I believe that people who learn to accept failure eventually become losers and that is a frame of mind that we should never accept. Be enthusiastic about trying new techniques but don't settle for anything less than success.

There are times when even the most experienced anglers start to get complacent or even bored with the status of their angling experiences. There are many causes of this dilemma. Some of us fall into the "three pound" funk where we start settling for fish less than that weight as our standard. Others simply get tired of catching the same old species using the same old techniques day after day. If you feel yourself falling into this kind of malaise, it's probably time for you to go back to basics in order to refresh your memory about the simpler aspect of angling. Let me relate a couple of short stories that might provide a better example.

In my book "The Catfish Hunters" I wanted to remind my readers that despite all the baits and lures that we carry, the earth worm and night crawler will forever remain the favorite food of every freshwater fish. I used the following example.

A friend named Stan Salzman who lived in Washington Park Illinois was fishing in a small barrow near his home. A barrow is usually a drainage pond that is constructed when a new development or a new highway is being built. Its purpose is to collect and hold drainage water keeping it away from the construction site. This barrow had been in place for many years and Salzman often fished there for catfish.

It had been raining for several days and the barrow was near its capacity. Salzman caught a 5 pound channel catfish which he felt was a nice size fish for that facility. He noticed however that the fish had an exceptionally large stomach. Since he had intended to eat this fish for dinner that evening, he wanted to take a closer look at the contents of the stomach. When he cut the fish open he was amazed at what he found. He put the stomach contents in a bowl to wash them so that he could take the photo shown below.

The fish was stuffed with earth worms, night crawlers and a couple of undigested crawfish. Many of the worms were still alive and Salzman decided to pick out the live ones to use as his bait the next day. The co-author of that book, Mac Byrum and I discussed this matter for some time. We had both done a lot of catfishing but neither of us ever used worms as our catfish bait. From that point forward, we decided to go back to basics with worms as one of our primary catfish baits.

But wait!, there's more to be learned here. Salzman told us that the contents shown above represented about one third of the stomach contents. The rest of the contents were mostly digested and they washed down the drain when he was rinsing them, but, the lost material was the same as that shown. What does this tell us about the eating habits of this catfish? First, as a drain basin, this barrow collected all of the worms that had been washed from the roadway during the previous three days of rain. The crawfish were probably residents of the barrow but the worms were the recently washed-in guests. Someone had probably put a few small channel catfish in the barrow years ago because it would take that long for a channel catfish to grow to five pounds. Following the days of rain, the catfish was gorging himself on the newly arrived food. Also take note that most of the non-digested worms are whole and intact. This indicates that the catfish didn't nibble on pieces of the worms it simply inhaled them live and whole. The same appears to be true for the crawfish. Most game fish have the same eating habits once they see an eating opportunity they inhale it and let their stomach do the heavy work. Perhaps it might be interesting during a feeding frenzy to toss a few TUMS overboard to help the fish along with the digestion process.

A couple of years ago, I found myself feeling like I needed a new fishing experience. My writer's organization SEOPA (Southeast Outdoor Writers Association) was holding its annual meeting at Fontana Lake in the middle of the Great Smoky Mountains of North Carolina. Among the pre conference activities was an opportunity to try some mountain stream trout fishing. I hadn't done any serious trout fishing in years and I was anxious to try a mountain stream again. A local fisherman named Danny Williams was assigned as my guide. I would be joined by Ed Wall, an outdoor writer for the New Bern Sun Journal newspaper.

It was a rainy morning and at one point I thought that the rain would cancel our day. Williams arrived a couple hours late asking if we still wanted to fish. Both Ed and I responded positively. Williams asked if we wanted to fish in a natural stream that was loaded with rainbow and brown trout, how could we resist that. My only concern, not knowing the conditions was that I had no waders or fly fishing gear.

Williams introductory welcome was to inform us that were going to fish along the back roads of Appalachia. I wasn't sure exactly how to interpret that comment because most of what I had heard or read about that region was not too inviting. I remember once reading that this part of the country was beautiful and the society was broken. Portions of the region were labeled the Big White Ghetto. The Appalachia region was a vast area extending north from Mississippi all the way to New York. At one point in history the residents of this region made their living harvesting and processing lumber and other natural resources. As the need for those resources disappeared, the entire region slowly went into a state of serious poverty.

Several government programs provided some help for the region. One such program was the construction of the Fontana Dam. This 480 foot dam impounds the Little Tennessee River and is the tallest dam east of the Rocky Mountains. The Alcoa Company of America was manufacturing aluminum for the war effort in the early 1940's. Their plant was in Alcoa Tennessee and their rapid expansion required more electric power that was available. Through Government backed efforts with the Tennessee Valley Authority the Fontana dam project was born. Also on December 28, 1942, President Roosevelt authorized the atomic bomb facility at Oak Ridge Tennessee and a population growth of more than 30,000 engineers and scientists, along with the Fontana Dam construction workers, flooded this area with jobs and growth in wealth. The housing facilities that were rapidly built for these workers eventually became what is today known as Fontana Village with the dam forming Fontana Lake. Although that small area has now grown as a resort area, the remainder of the Appalachia region remains in poverty.

We hopped into Williams' truck and he drove about ten miles north of Fontana. Williams finally pulled off the road in a fairly well developed area with several houses scattered along the road. "Where's the stream" I asked, "Just tother side of them bushes" he responded as he took a couple of light spinning rods from the truck bed. Each rod was equipped with a very small hook and a small split shot weight. Williams opened a white foam cup that was full of worms, handing each of us a piece about half inch long. "Push your way through the bushes find a small pool of water and drop the worm in, you'll catch a trout in every pool".

The stream in that particular area was less than two feet wide and that was a high water level due to the overnight rains. In most areas there were bushes on both sides of the stream so getting to the water itself was somewhat of a challenge. I moved a short distance downstream and saw a very small pool of slower water. I dropped my baited hook into the pool and soon caught a nine inch rainbow trout shown below.

I immediately realized that these fish were hungry and we were going to damage them with the barbed hooks that we were using so I asked Williams for a set of pliers so I could bend in the barb so as not to damage the fish. From that point on the challenge became more difficult because it was easy for the fish to toss the hook, which was exactly what we wanted.

Because of the nature of the stream and the conditions of the surrounding bushes, in short time my feet were soaked as were my pants and shirt. My hands and arms showed signs of the thorns that were everywhere. This was more than back to basics fishing, this was primitive fishing, but this was the way it all started for me and I loved every minute of it.

In a three hour period I caught about fifteen trout and managed to keep nearly all of them alive to bite again on another angler's line. The few fish that we felt would not survive were gladly packed away by Williams for his next day's lunch. All told Wall and I caught about thirty fish and only three were questionable survivors.

One interesting aspect of this experience was that the stream we fished ran along a main road and across the front yard of many resident houses. Williams indicated that none of the residents minded anglers fishing the stream, but I realized that was probably because he knew every one of these people by name, even familiar with the names of their dogs. Had Ed Wall and I come here alone, we might have gotten a different reception.

The widest and most scenic area of the stretch of stream that we fished is shown below. With few thorns and some trimmed bushes, it was the easiest to fish but guess what neither Wall nor I caught any fish in this area. What's that tell you about the areas that fish like to hide?

I have to admit that the three hours of Smoky Mountain trout fishing has carved a place in my memory, more than many other fishing experiences where I caught more and bigger fish. There are no mounted fish in my memories room from this fishing experience but it restored my passion for the very basics of fishing and made me more appreciative of all the other opportunities that I have. This was truly **Fishing Different.**

I made the statement earlier that there are only three significant causes of changes in fish behavior. These causes are the condition of the water in which the fish live, the availability of an adequate food source and the position and penetration of the sun. All other factors that have been advertised as causes of changing behavior are only secondary effects. From this point on in this book I will provide the details of my theories on these subjects.

Chapter Three

Understanding the Waters in Which the Fish Live

"Accepting the conventional wisdom serves to protect us from the painful job of thinking."

John Kenneth Galbraith

I hinted in some earlier pages, that the rapidly changing cultures and habits of the newer generations seems to be proving that thinking is a very painful activity. As such it often seems as if simply accepting the status quo is far easier than looking at current facts and reasoning a conclusion.

There are a number of myths that have been handed down over the years that have become very popular among even the most avid anglers. If one is to understand the science of fishing it is necessary to also grasp the science from whence these myths evolved. Since that has been my objective for many years, I have discovered that some of these "guiding concepts" are no longer valid when tested against the modern science that we practice today. The following chapters will discuss these theories, myths, and concepts in detail. You may find my conclusions and theories radical and even disturbing, because they might cause you to start Fishing Different.

A common statement that is made about just about every water body is that 90% of the fish are located in 10% of the water area. That statement I have found to be true, but it is not surprising. Let's compare the surrounding of a fish to the surroundings of we humans.

As a former pilot, I have flown over a large portion of this country and as I looked down where I could see for many miles in all directions, I realized that the same startling fact is true for humans. Across this vast landscape of millions of square miles, 80% of the population lives in 20% of the land mass of this country. Why is this? It's because most of the country is covered with mountains, forests and desert where it is hard to get around or the climate is simply too severe for human existence. Think about the areas where the 80% live. They live near water sources like rivers and oceans or near metropolitan areas where work and business are plentiful. Of course we can always find someone living in the wilderness or in the hot desert, but those situations are rare. As this country developed and grew, factories were located near rivers and streams as a source of energy. The factories provided jobs for the people so the people moved close to where their work was located. That's why most large cities are located near a water source: for jobs, shipping, and transportation.

So like humans, fish, when looking for a place to live, will seek out areas that provide them specific solutions to their survival needs like the availability of food sources and places to hide or seek shelter from the elements.

The Importance of Structure

In my experience, the most important element of any water body that offers fish what they are seeking is structure. Structure comes in many forms beneath the surface of the water. Most people think of structure in terms of physical mass. I don't think in those terms. Of course physical mass is in fact structure, but another form of structure that is rarely thought of in those terms is topographical structure which is simply a rapid change or variation of the bottom formation under the water. These are nature's structures like drop offs, humps, rock formations, underwater points and shoals and deep crevasses. These topographical structures are often more important for fish habitat than physical structures.

Physical structures like logs, trees, underwater growth, docks, and bridges are important for several reasons. In most waters, physical structures will eventually collect algae, which is a source of food for the micro-life that lives in the water called plankton. These tiny live organisms feed on the algae and they in turn become the food for the newly hatched small fish and bait fish. Wherever the bait fish congregate, the predator fish are soon to follow.

Another important aspect of physical structure is it provides a place for fish to hide or gain cover. Most of the common game fish are born with the instinct to hide from other larger fish that are also always looking for something to eat. This instinct usually drives fish to seek a hiding place where they are not quite as visible to their predators. Conversely, many predator fish like bass, will use physical structure to hide from their prey that they are looking to attack and eat.

Another important factor involving structure like docks and bridges is that they provide a place for the fish to get out of penetrating sunlight. I will address sunlight in other areas of this book, but in my opinion sunlight is a big enemy of all fish and a very important issue for anglers. Look at nearly all game-type fish and there are two things they all have in common. Their eyes are near the top of their head and those eyes are usually pointed upward. Also, fish have no eye lids so they have no way to shut out heavy sun rays like we humans do. I can remember one incident where I visited my ophthalmologist for my annual check-up. The nurse dilated my eyes for the examination and when I left the office to go to my car the bright sun was terribly painful to my eyes. I had to nearly completely close my eyes to reach my car. When I did reach the car, having no sun glasses, I had to wait nearly an hour to reopen my eyes so I could safely drive home. Fish have no eye lids so the only way they can prevent the discomfort of direct sunlight is to get behind something that blocks the sun from them. Physical structure provides the fish that shading mechanism.

Topographical structure is normally provided by nature with its natural fluctuations in bottom formations. Almost any radical change in bottom formation provides an attraction to fish. Drop-offs, underwater points, and shoals are popular gathering places for schools of small bait fish. These small creatures were given the instinct at birth to hide from anything bigger than themselves. They normally travel in schools and when they feel threatened, they will often head for a place that they think protects them from attack from at least one side and they crowd up against some form of wall, like a sharp drop-off. In fact when they do this they are simply cutting off one of their avenues of escape when predators come looking for them. Crevasses in the bottom landscape have the same effect except that in these situations the bait schools have virtually locked themselves into a two-walled trap. Almost any significant change in bottom landscape is always a place for fish to congregate.

One of the reasons most freshwater fish are caught less than 100 feet from a shoreline is that this is normally the area where structure or landscape changes are located. Wind, rain and land erosion will cause trees to fall into the water adding more physical structure. Docks and other man-made structures are nearly always located on or close to land. It has always caused me to chuckle that professional anglers frown on fishing from shore but they will launch their $60,000 boats and speed to an area to fish that is less than 25 feet off shore, casting their lures into very shallow water and around docks and other man-made physical structure. Why do they do this? They do it because that's where the fish are living. The boat in these instances is only a mechanism to get the angler from one area of docks to another, or from one underwater point or hump to another one.

There are other factors that will influence the best location for fish in a specific body of water. The presence of underwater and shoreline plant growth is also very important. Bass specifically like areas where there is under-water plant life. Grass or lily pads are an indication that fish will be in the area. If there are areas where a fresh water supply is feeding the lake, this will normally be marked by fresh green growth near the shoreline. These areas normally signal higher oxygen content to the water and will attract fish of all species. Areas below dams or below small waterfalls are also areas of higher oxygen content. Large boulder formations along the shoreline or even protruding through the water surface in off-shore locations are good indicators of residing fish. Shaded areas and areas of fallen trees would be good areas to look for fish. Watch the shoreline for Blue Heron activity. These predators will hang out where they know there are small fish. Gull and loon activity is also a signal of the presence of small bait fish. In areas where there are active eagles or osprey, these birds will often build their nests in areas where they know there are fish as their food supply. All of these indicators can be used to provide you easier access to those 10% areas where the fish are located and will provide you with a higher probability of catching fish.

Temperature Considerations

The "bathtub theory" which I described briefly in the introduction is used extensively as an example by a close friend of mine, to attempt to explain to beginners to our sport the idea of finding the fish. The theory is quite simple. You can fill your bath tub with water, find a comfortable chair and sit by that tub all day long with your line in the water and you will never catch any fish. The reason is easy to understand, there simply are no fish in that tub. Sounds silly doesn't it? Yet time and again I hear folks tell me that they can't catch fish in one or another lake or pond and when we talk for a while I realize it is because they have little or no understanding of where the fish might be located or how they behave under different circumstances.

In my earlier books I went into considerable detail on water body theory and fish biology to help explain how and why fish behave as they do. Perhaps I got a little too detailed in those descriptions causing my readers not to grasp the true meaning of my comments. I'll attempt here to use another approach that may be easier to understand. This approach is based upon simple logic. I am an engineer and engineers are often criticized for being too pragmatic, meaning that they base too many of their decision on logic and common sense. That criticism is probably true and because of it, I am hesitant to suggest that everyone use a little more common sense when thinking about finding the fish. As I discuss the changing cultures with friends and associates, I am becoming somewhat alarmed that much of the upcoming generations have problems rationalizing decisions. It seems that it's just easier to Google a question than it is to think it out. But I guess that just another problem caused by the tremendous technological progress with computers and other information devices. As a future "old timer" I'll just have to adapt to that change.

Let's use some common sense here. During the course of my life, and probably safe to say the course of many previous generations, animal life has not changed. Dogs are still dogs; they look and act the same as they always have. Wildlife like deer and bear has never changed, one is hunted as a food source and the other is still feared. The fish hook has not changed in concept in 42,000 years and fish are still fish, they still live in water, they still need oxygen to survive and their principle motivation in life is for survival. To survive they must eat and try not to be eaten and they must continue to procreate their species. These motives have never changed as far back as history has been recorded, and probably never will change.

If we think about those motivations it will help us think out the process of finding where fish live and when they eat. Let's think of the fish as we think of ourselves as humans. Humans are warm blooded and we need to keep that blood within certain temperature limits to be comfortable. When the air surrounding us gets cold we are able to put on additional clothes to regain comfort and bring our blood up to the correct temperature. Fish are cold blooded creatures and when their surroundings change temperature, they can't add clothing or other insulation. But nature has provided for that by permitting the fish to change their metabolism within their body. When the surroundings are exceptionally cold, their metabolism slows down, they move around much slower and they eat much less. Like we humans, in winter months when it's terribly cold outside, even with the ability to add clothing, we tend to avoid being out in the cold and if we are required to be outside, we tend to move slower and our body lets us know when we are about to freeze if we don't react to the weather.

Similarly when our surroundings get very warm in the hot summer months, we sometimes shed some clothing, but more often we seek cooler temperatures inside a structure. If we have to stay in the hot temperature, we slow down our movements and our entire brain works slightly differently. Similarly, there is also a high temperature where fish become uncomfortable and in some cases that temperature gets so hot that the fish die. They are not able, as we are, to go inside where it cooler. Their only recourse to hot water is to find cover and go deeper in the water where the temperature is a little cooler. In this situation they are also less active than they are when in comfortable water temperatures. The comfort zones are different for different fish species. The illustration below shows the temperature limits for several common game fish.

Lake Norman Fish Preferred Water Temperatures (Degrees F)				
Species	Lower Limit	Upper Limit	Optimum	Most Active
Largemouth	50	85	73	65-75
Spotted bass	50	82	71	60-70
Striper	50	75	65	55-65
Catfish Flathead	60	90	75	70-80
Catfish Blue	55	90	70	65-80
Catfish Channel	65	90	75	70-80
Crappie	55	90	65	60-78
Common Carp	70	95	80	79-85
White Perch	55	95	70	65-80
Gar	65	95	85	80-90
Bream	60	90	75	70-80

The lower temperature limit average for most fish appears to be around 50 degrees F with the upper limit around 90 degrees F. The optimum average temperature level seems to be around 75 degrees F. One thing we must always remember, fish are very adaptable creatures so we should never consider these numbers as absolute. In the south, as an example, where the temperatures are normally higher for longer periods of the year, fish will adjust to these temperatures because they have no choice. Similarly in the northern regions where the colder months extend through more months of the year, the fish will also adapt to that variation.

A very important factor that is closely associated with the water temperature is the oxygen content of the water. If the oxygen content is higher because the area receives more rain fall, or there are water diversions like dams or waterfalls, these areas will attract the fish because fish want the higher oxygen content water. There is a fairly constant relationship between water temperature and oxygen content as shown below.

Average Minimum Oxygen Reqirements		
Water Temp	Maximun DO	Minimum DO Reqd.
41 deg F	12.8 mg/l	9.1 mg/l
50 deg F	11.3 mg/l	8.8 mg/l
59 deg F	10.2 mg/l	8.3 mg/l
68 deg F	9.2 mg/l	7.8 mg/l
77 deg F	8.2 mg/l	7.5 mg/l
86 deg F	7.4 mg/l	6.9 mg/l

I have found that fish react more to the oxygen content of the water than they do to the temperature in terms of their activity level. Remember what I said earlier comparing fish behavior to human behavior. Think about how humans react to reductions in the oxygen supply, when we fly on commercial airlines above the oxygen level at 10,000 feet, we need to have oxygen mixed into the cabin air. When athletes perform in the higher elevations of states like Colorado, their efficiency is significantly reduced. Fish react the same way except that in many cases there is no way for the fish to adjust the oxygen concentration. Fish oxygenate their bodies by gas absorption in their gills, but if there is little oxygen in the water, none is available for absorption. At very low oxygen levels (below 3.0 mg/L) fish are severely stressed and many species will die.

Another aspect of water temperature that has a big effect on an angler's ability to catch fish is the behavior of the small bait fish that are the prey and food for the predator fish. Smaller and younger fish have a greater reaction to water temperature changes because their systems are not as adaptable. A one or two degree F change in water temperature might not be too serious to a large predator fish, but it is significant to the small fish. The chart below illustrates the desired temperatures of a few of the more popular bait fish.

Lake Norman Bait Fish Preferred Water Temp(°F)	
Species	Preferred Water temp (°F)
Gizzard Shad	63-80
Threadfin Shad	50-85
Herring	50-70
Common Shiner	65-85
Golden Shiner	70-80
White Perch	65-80

Upon initial examination, the desired temperature ranges are very close to the desired temperatures of the larger game fish. The different however is that the small bait fish will react sooner to temperature changes. As the water gets warmer during the summer months, the bait will almost immediately go deeper to find the cooler water. In the winter when the water surface temperature drops significantly, the bait fish will also seek the deeper water because in the winter months the water is warmer as it becomes deeper.

There is data available that shows the variations in water temperature with variations in water depth. There are many factors that influence that data, like the amount of current or water flow, and how quickly the water temperature rises or falls, but I have found that a good average relationship for a large relatively deep lake is a temperature variation of one and one half degree F for every ten feet of water depth. So in the hot summer months when the surface temperature is high, the temperature will be 1½ degree cooler for every ten feet deeper that it is measured. Similarly in the cold winter months, the same relationship exists except that for every ten feet of depth, the water temperature will get 1½ degrees F warmer. The large schools of bait fish will react to a 2 or 3 degree change in water temperature faster that the larger fish will react. So when the water temperature suddenly gets hotter or colder, the bait fish will retreat to the deeper water and of course the predators will realize that exodus and follow them, even though the larger fish may be able to tolerate the change more easily. A good criterion for locating fish in any large water body is to follow the food source. In cold months of November, December and January, the fish will be deep. In the spring and fall months when the temperatures are stable, the fish will be in the shallower water and in the hot summer months of July and August, the fish will again be deeper, but possibly not quite as deep as in the cold winter months.

CHAPTER FOUR

The Myth About Barometric Pressure

"Conformity is the father of freedom and the enemy of growth."

President John F. Kennedy

It was only through archaeological discoveries that we learned of the first fish hook discovered by a Neanderthal, possibly named Gronk, more than 42,000 years ago. More recent recorded history tells of many actual inventions and discoveries as late as the 1600's that even today help separate fact from fiction about basic fishing lore. Many of the more important early discoveries were made by a man named Blaise Pascal. To better understand the brilliance of some of the important scientists of past centuries it might help to take a quick look at a few of these important people.

Blaise Pascal was born in France on June 19, 1623. He was educated by his father who realized his potential genius and didn't want to chance the normal educational system to bring out this capability. At the very early age of sixteen Pascal formulated one of the most basic theories of projected geometry. In 1642 Pascal's father was having great difficulty with all of the calculations needed to determine the amount of taxes he owed so Blaise invented the first mechanical adding machine. Because his friend was having difficulty understanding the theories associated with gambling, Pascal provided the needed information that led to today's modern theory of probability. In 1648 he provided Evangelista Torricelli the critical proof needed to develop the Barometer.

As indicated by President Kennedy's statement above, there are times when people get into the habit of just falling in line with conventional thinking, just accepting something that was presented years ago as fact and accepted by society without challenge. Then along comes someone who takes the time to think further about that subject and finds that the premise of the original idea might be wrong, making the entire theory wrong. These new ideas are the seeds of growth in knowledge.

So is the case when it comes to the subject of barometric pressure and its effect on the behavior of fish. It's nearly impossible to read of an interview with a professional angler without hearing their theory about barometric pressure and how it has such a great influence on the behavior of fish. Since I was old enough to read about fishing tales, I had been led to believe that a day with low barometric pressure creates good fishing conditions and a day with high barometric pressure makes for bad fishing. Like millions of others I simply accepted this premise because it had been around so long that I felt it just must be true.

The subject of barometric pressure was brought to the forefront of my mind as a pilot where the barometer carries great important to aviators because it tells them the altitude of the aircraft. For a long time I was bothered by the fact that barometric pressure changed the behavior of fish, or at least that is what all anglers believed. I would sometimes get flash backs of my high school physics class, where I first learned that barometric pressure was discovered and is measured by a standard that starts at sea level and changes as altitude above sea level changes. Why were the fishing experts now using this measure beneath the surface of the water? "This is not valid" I thought and in my first book, "Jakes Take on The Lake." I pronounced for the first time that barometric pressure as a causal factor had little to do with the behavior of fish. It was my recollection that below the surface of the water the hydrostatic pressure was the variant that might indeed cause fish to change their behavior and the variant that caused changes in hydrostatic pressure was the depth of the water, not barometric pressure.

Since I was now putting myself into a public position on this subject, I decided to look back at the basic physics that underlies this subject and I have altered my original position, but, not my conclusions. Since I continue to publically state that barometric pressure has little to do with the changes in fish behavior, I went back and did considerable research on the subject to make sure that my claims could be supported by basic science. In my later book, "Beneath The Surface," I published the detailed science and mathematics that support my conclusions. I have presented that detail in Appendix 1 of this book.

I am providing the details as an appendix because I believe that the average reader is prepared to accept my conclusions without wading through the math. If however, someone wants to get on my band wagon supporting my argument, the details in the appendix will provide them supporting information to prove the thesis.

To take my theory a bit farther, I have prepared two tables shown below to illustrate how hydrostatic pressure varies with water depth and how total underwater pressure varies with a range of variations in barometric pressure.

Total pressure changes vs.barometric pressure changes at 10 feet depth			Hydrostatic pressure changes with water depth at std. atm.29.92	
Barometric Pressure	Hydrostatic Pressure (PSI)	Percent Change	Water Depth	Hydrostatic Pressure
			1 Ft.	15.10 psi
29.92	19.039	0%	2 Ft.	15.53 psi
29.93	19.034	.02%	3 Ft.	15.96 psi
29.94	19.0479	.04%	4 Ft.	16.01 psi
29.95	19.0528	.06%	5 Ft.	16.83 psi
29.96	19.0577	.08%	6 Ft.	17.28 psi
29.97	19.0626	.10%	7 Ft.	17.70 psi
29.98	19.0675	.12%	8 Ft.	18.13 psi
29.99	19.0724	.14%	9 Ft.	18.55 psi
30.00	19.0773	.16%	10 Ft.	19.00 psi
30.01	19.0822	.19%		
30,02	19.0871	.20%		
30.03	19.0920	.30%		
30.04	19.0979	.40%		

What these tables illustrate is that a wide variation in barometric pressure has almost negligible effect on hydrostatic pressure, less than four tenths of one percent. The big variable that does have an effect is water depth where a 10 foot change in depth causes nearly a 25% change in pressure.

Another common measure of Barometric Pressure is a unit of measurecalled millibars. Conversion charts are readily available if one desires to use this measure, but I do not consider it relevant here.

There is a great deal of written material on how fish behavior changes significantly as the barometric pressure changes. Most fishermen have subscribed to the theory that falling and low pressure increase the bite and rising and high pressure lessen the bite. Although these writings are interesting and have given cause for many fishermen over the years to change their fishing habits to accommodate pressure changes, few if any of these writings have described why fish behavior changes. The reason there has never been a meaningful explanation of why the change occurs is that in fact it does not occur.

To further verify my theory, I decided to start tracking my fish catches as they related to the changes in barometric pressure. I only used data from fishing days where I fished the entire day and then compared my catch rates to the changes in pressure that had occurred during those times. I recorded the barometric pressure every hour on a portable barometer and then cross checked those measurements with the historical pressure recorded in local weather records. One such five day fishing trip is shown below.

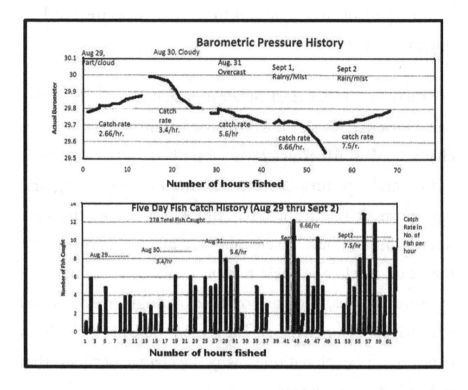

What become obvious from this data is that my catch rate increased each day regardless of the rising or dropping barometric pressure. It should be noted, however, that on each day of this trip, the sun rarely if ever shined. Fishing was good during dropping pressure and it was good during rising pressure tending to confirm my theory that it is the sunlight that really has the effect on fish behavior, not barometric pressure. I have collected additional data for several other fishing trips and have several charts that depict the same results that I did not include in this book.

Some recent publications, more specifically a book titled "The Barometric Breakthrough," written by Andrew Bett of Great Britain, provides a great deal of discussion and supporting data that the author concludes presents a completely different argument about the pressure issue. Bett concludes the exact opposite from the conventional wisdom of American anglers that rises in barometric pressure make for better fishing and drops in pressure decreases the bite. Bett uses Trout and Salmon as his fish species and his data provides conclusions from very few actual data points. If measured against US standards, the sparse data used by Bett would not be considered to be a statistically valid sample, but it was significant enough in the UK to cause publication of an entire book dedicated to his conclusions.

Bett, like a few American writers, uses reference sources that feel that the behavioral changes in fish result from the existence of a "swim bladder," "float bladder," or "air bladder" in most freshwater fish. This bladder allows a fish to achieve neutral buoyancy at different depths by increasing or decreasing the amount of air in the bladder. Different types of fish regulate this air flow in different ways and there are a few fish that actually have no such bladder, namely the shark. Fish without a float bladder need to use their swimming ability to change their position in the water column. If they stop swimming, they will sink to the bottom due to the lack of internal buoyancy.

The "bladder theorists" claim that changes in the barometric pressure cause the fish's bladder to react to these changes, which in turn causes the fish to react differently. As I have stated above, significant changes in barometric pressure would only have a minute effect on the hydrostatic pressure applied to the fish and this pressure change is so small that the fish can accommodate it by changing their depth only a few inches, hardly significant. I'll discuss the swim bladder in more detail later in this section.

In my book, "Jakes take on The Lake," I discuss this phenomenon concluding that barometric pressure has no "causal" relationship to fish behavior, but that it is the weather related factors that accompany barometric pressure, namely the existence and position of sunlight and its ability to penetrate the water depths that effects fish behavior. In general, low pressure days bring overcast skies and hide the sun and high pressure days result in good weather and a brighter sunshine. My second book, "Freshwater

Fighters," provides some very comprehensive data on this subject, which resulted from fish catches numbering several hundred fish. These results are certainly more statistically valid than data that has been presented by others.

I have concluded that weather itself is the cause of behavioral changes in fish, not pressure. Wind, as an example breaks the surface and deflects the sunlight. Wind, if sustained, also causes small currents where they might not otherwise occur causing movements in the bait schools and also, at times, causing fish to change their normal (at rest) pointing direction. Fishermen, who troll for fish, will notice that the bite is often better in one direction than it is in the other direction due to this pointing issue.

Rain, normally associated with low pressure, causes changes in the oxygen levels in the water and will often bring fish closer to the surface for a better oxygen supply. Rain also washes new nutrients into the water bringing fish closer to shore to feed.

Temperature changes resulting from passage of cold or warm fronts can have a significant effect on water temperature, which we know changes the behavioral patterns of fish, perhaps more than any other weather element.

All of these weather related factors do indeed change the behavior of fish and they are all normally associated with changes in barometric pressure that accompany the weather. It is the weather factors, mostly the penetration of the sun, not the barometric pressure that is the culprit.

Since there seems to be some science related to the "bladder theory" I thought I should at least take a harder look at the workings of the swim bladder to see if I could find some credible evidence that a swim bladder could indeed detect minute changes in pressure.

Paleoichthyologists believe that the very earliest fish had no swim bladders. Even today, a few species have survived with no such bladders. Sharks, rays and eels have no swim bladders and they must use their bodies to swim to the water depth that they desire and remain there. If these fish stop swimming, they will sink to the bottom and remain there until they again swim to other depths. This, of course, is because a fish is heavier than the water that it is in. Freshwater has a density of 1.0 and a typical fish has a density of 1.076, hence under normal resting conditions the fish would slowly sink to the bottom.

Nature has performed wonderful acts on animals as well as humans. Since swimming, all of the time, to stay off the bottom is expensive in terms of energy needed and resting on the bottom is normally not practical, nature had to evolve a solution to this problem. The solution was the evolution of the swim bladder. The swim bladder is a gas filled bag that sits in the body cavity of a fish, above all of the other organs. It is placed high in the body cavity to give buoyancy to the fish. The evolution of the swim bladder freed the fish: they no longer had to keep moving in order to stay at the level in the water that they wanted to be at. They could now use their fins to help them perform more complicated maneuvers like staying still, swimming slowly, swimming head down or head up or even swimming backwards.

The swim bladder of some fish is an ellipsoidal, gas filled sac that arises as an extension of the gut and the fish can use this connection to control the amount of gas in the swim bladder. Fish with this type of bladder connection live mostly in shallow water and often take in air by swallowing it at the surface. This air is then passed through the gut and then forced into the swim bladder. In other species, mostly those fish that live in deeper water (most sport fishing species) the connection to the gut is closed off and no gas can move from the gut to the swim bladder. These fish are able to control the amount of gas in the swim bladder, by means of several areas on the walls of the bladder that are very thin and contain capillaries to pass the gas through the bladder wall.

The ability to control the amount of gas in the swim bladder is essential because this is the only way that the fish can control its buoyancy and remain at a particular depth in the water. Since the amount of gas in the bladder will only keep the fish buoyant at one depth, the fish must alter this gas if it desires to settle at another depth.

We have seen from the chart above illustrating depth and pressure relationships that there is significant pressure change with water depth caused by the water pressure alone. This is why a fish choosing to rise from any significant depth to the surface must release air bubbles while rising in the water column. It is not unusual for large catfish, as an example, if quickly pulled from deeper water, to have an extended bladder that is visible and on occasion can protrude from its mouth. If this excess gas is not released before the fish is back in the water, it will not be able to submerge to its desires depth and on occasion the fish will die at the surface.

The illustration below shows one such situation where a Catfish bladder is visibly protruding from its side. It was necessary to "burp" this fish by inserting the anglers hand and finger into the throat to permit the release of the gas and the fish was safely released.

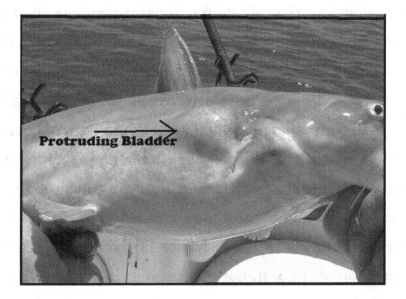

So, we now understand the purpose and functioning of the swim bladder for buoyancy control, but how is it also the control mechanism for changing the behavior of the fish as the barometric pressure changes? The answer? It is not.

Nowhere in my reading of more than two dozen writings on the swim bladder is mention ever made of any effect of barometric pressure or the use of the bladder to adjust for barometric pressure changes. Most game fish of the type normally sought by sport anglers will freely and regularly move through 10 or 15 feet changes in depth in the course of daily feeding activity. As I have shown above, the pressure changes that the fish witness in these normal transitions are far greater than the minute fractional percentage changes in pressure caused by barometric pressure changes at the surface. A pressure change of five or six hundredths of a percent would not even be detected by the swim bladder and could be compared to a human taking a normal breath. I believe that I have done enough basic mathematics and taken enough practical data to permit my conclusion that we can forget about barometric pressure changes as the cause for changes in the behavior of game fish. It's the penetration of the sun, not the barometric pressure that is the culprit.

When we argue about the relative merits of barometric pressure it might be worth asking why professional anglers do not carry a barometer as standard equipment in their boats. If they were so convinced of the effect of this pressure, it would seem logical that they would carry this equipment with them at all times, as I did when I was collecting the data previously presented.

Most of my curiosity about barometric pressure stems from my memory of those days of High School physics when I learned how the barometer was discovered. Evangelista Torricelli has been credited with the invention of the barometer in 1643, but some historians believe that Gaspara Berti actually discovered the water barometer between 1640 and 1643. There were problems with the water barometer theories and it wasn't until 1646 that Torricelli consulted with (guess who) his friend Blaise Pascal and Pascal suggested that atmospheric pressure, not a water vacuum, was causing their crude barometer to change readings. Pascal also introduced the theory that air weighed less at high altitudes which eventually led to the invention of the aircraft altimeter. For those anglers who have permitted barometric pressure to govern their fishing habits, I suggest that they simply start **fishing different.**

CHAPTER FIVE

The Water: It's About More Than Temperature

"We keep moving forward, opening new doors and doing new things, because we're curious and curiosity keeps leading us down new paths."

Walt Disney

There are times that we all have some degree of difficulty comprehending the history of our own planet which credible scholars have indicated was born 4.54 billion years ago. We know that looking back that far, the earth didn't look like it does today. Several continents were linked together and it was billions of years later that the global situation changed to what it is today.

In terms of the oceans and the live creatures that lived there, we have been told that the first known shark existence dates back to the Devonian period around 370 million years ago and some biologic life forms date back as far as 3.5 billion years.

The first primates, a life form that had vertebrae and used its fingers and toes, date back about 50 to 55 million years. This is more than 10 million years after the dinosaurs became extinct. The first known fish-like creature was the Pikaia, the first water life to exist having vertebrae. The Pikaia was probably 2 inches long and translucent and possibly existed around 500 million years ago.

I started this book by offering the possibility that Gronk, the Neanderthal, was the first living thing to begin the discoveries that led to today's modern fishing techniques. The Neanderthals were considered to be a sub-species of humans since their DNA was 98% similar to human DNA. Give or take a million years that means that more than 500 million years passed before we started to understand the seas and the creatures that inhabited them.

We are still trying to hone that knowledge today so it not unusual that because of man's curiosity, discoveries are still being made that will help fill the gaps in knowledge about the earth's waters and the life forms that inhabited them. The study of nature continues to lead us down new paths keeping us moving forward.

Most anglers understand the importance of water temperature. That's why I put that subject up front in Chapter Three. There is much more to the surrounding waters in which a fish spends it entire life than simply the water temperature. The ability of freshwater fish to live healthily and grow at their ideal rate is a function of six factors: water quality; nutrients in the food and water; seasonal weather variations; available food sources; competition for the food, and fishing pressure. Each of these factors has a slightly different effect on different species of fish so I will generalize for simplicity.

In recent decades living near the water has become an element for human quality of life. As a result many waters have become more developed and this growth in development has created a conflict concerning water quality in terms of what is best for the health of aquatic life. Residents would like their lake and stream water to be pure and absent of any pollutants. Fish and other aquatic life living in these waters will not flourish in pure water because they require certain nutrients for a healthy life.

In many of our far northern lakes that are considered wilderness waters, there has been no development. The quality of the water in these lakes is completely controlled by nature. These waters are generally clear of any waste products except those that are provided by other wildlife. The waters contain many nutrients that are washed in by wind, rain and melting snow. Most anglers enjoy fishing these waters because they normally produce large, healthy fish.

In developed waters, pollutants are caused by both direct and indirect point sources. Direct sources are the outflows and pipes that bring pollution sources directly to our lakes and rivers. Roadways, paved parking lots and storm drains eventually find their way into pipes that flow into these waters. Indirect sources provide the greatest amount of pollution. These sources are fertilizers, herbicides, oil, grease, salt, pet waste, and agricultural run-off. The two damaging pollutants that result from both these sources are PCP (polychlorinated biphenyls) and mercury. There are a number of state and federal agencies that have the responsibility for monitoring and controlling the pollution problem, but the largest single controlling factor is nature itself. Nature has as its goal to keep all of the various elements in balance. Unfortunately Nature is the least understood source for this control and we humans often take actions that work against nature's processes.

Major Sources of Nutrients in the Water

Nutrients are essential for the construction of healthy tissue in every living thing. Nutrients are a source of stored energy for digestion, growth, and reproduction. In other words, the proper concentration of nutrients available to fish supports every basic element of their survival. There is one significant difference in the nutrition requirements for fish and those of all other living creatures. Fish exist in an environment of neutral gravity. They are neutrally buoyant and therefore they do not need the heavy skeleton like other animals and mammals do. This significantly reduces the level of calcium and phosphorous that fish need for healthy growth. Because of this neutral buoyancy, fish also need less nutrition to support locomotion since fish use less energy for moving themselves around in the water than animals and humans that live on land.

Nutrition is critical to fish health because it provides energy, permits growth, and prevents disease. Nutrients are available to fish either through the food they eat or the water in which they live. It needs to be available in the proper proportions to support the fish within their specific living environment. As an example, fish living in water where the current is always fast, require more nutrition to support the extra energy they need to live naturally in these waters. Energy producing nutrients are mostly derived from carbohydrates. Sixty percent of a fish's energy comes from carbohydrates, 30% comes from fats, and 10% comes from protein. A fish that lives in relatively calm waters will probably require fewer carbohydrates in its diet because its existence requires less energy. The food requirement for fish varies greatly with the species of the fish, but in general terms, for normal growth, fish need to eat between 0.5% and 1.5% of their body weight each day.

The major sources of nutrients in lakes and rivers are precipitation, dissolution of natural minerals from soil, fertilizer application, and effluent from sewage plants. Let's look at each of these sources individually.

Precipitation. The earth's atmosphere is about 78 percent nitrogen. Most of this nitrogen is in the form of nitrogen gas. There are other compounds of nitrogen and oxygen that are generated by the chemical reactions resulting from the burning of fossil fuels. These compounds eventually find their way to form a nitrate which can be dissolved in rain water and snow and easily reach our streams and lakes.

Minerals. The largest reservoir of phosphorus in the environment is not in the atmosphere but in minerals in rocks, sediment, and soil. Where natural deposits of phosphorus minerals are mined, such as in Florida and Idaho, runoff and seepage is a major source of phosphorus in those water ways. Phosphorus compounds in general are much less soluble than nitrogen compounds and do not readily move into runoff or seepage.

Fertilizers. Development close to our rivers and lakes creates an environment where nitrogen and phosphorus in large quantities are contained in fertilizers. About 11 million tons of nitrogen and 2 million tons of phosphorus are applied to our soil annually through fertilizer. Another 6.5 million tons of nitrogen and 2 million tons of phosphorus are applied in manure. Much of this is runoff into our lakes and rivers.

Sewage effluent. Organic nitrogen, ammonia and organic phosphorus are present in sewage treatment plant effluents. In the three year period between 1978 and 1981, sewage treatment plants discharged about 13 million tons of nitrogen per year into our nation's waters. The Clean Water Act of 1972 has gone a long way to reducing the extent of this problem.

Seasonal Weather Variations

Because fish are cold-blooded organisms, the rate of growth of a fish is significantly affected by the length of the growing season. In Chapter Three I discussed the ideal temperatures for various species of fish. The growth rate of a specific species is fastest within those ideal temperature ranges. Some states have longer summer months where the ideal growth conditions exist for a long period whereas a colder northern state has a shorter growing season. Let's take one example. A typical walleye likes an average growing temperature between 55 and 65 degrees. A typical walleye in Kansas where the average water temperature is about 65 degrees, might take three years to grow to a length of 18 inches. That same walleye living in a Canadian lake where the average water temperature is about 55 degrees might take 15 years to grow to 18 inches.

This temperature effect on fish also clearly illustrates why certain species are normally found in the southern regions, like catfish that grow to huge sizes in the warm southern waters. This same species can live in the northern waters but it will not grow to the same large sizes in these cooler waters.

Available Food Sources

The most dominant factor influencing fish growth is, of course, the food that it eats, both in quantity and quality. It is possible to make a direct comparison between the eating habits of fish and those of humans. Humans who eat large quantities of food regularly will grow to larger sizes than those who control the extent of food intake. At the same time humans who eat large quantities of low quality foods will grow to heavier sizes but will not be as healthy as those who selectively eat more nutritious foods.

Fish, as part of their survival instinct, tend to eat all of the time. There is no regular eating time like breakfast or dinner for fish. Many anglers believe that shortly after sunrise and shortly before sunset are the most active feeding times and I will discuss that elsewhere in this book. Fish however, are opportunistic eaters and will eat whatever comes along, regardless of the quality of that food source. A water body that contains a well balanced source of aquatic life including both plants and other living creatures will contain fish that are larger and healthier than less balanced waters.

With the possible exception of carp, most game fish species will get the important protein that they need from other aquatic living creatures and these come in many forms.

Worms are a universal food for all fresh water fish. Whether live earthworms, grubs or red worms, these creatures are a very high protein source, they are available in and around all fresh waters, and they easily inhaled and digested by the fish. Bluegill and catfish are known to love worms, but all other species will also eat worms.

Amphibians, such as tadpoles, frogs, lizards, and crawfish are readily available as food for fish in every fresh water body. Bass, particularly small mouth bass. go crazy for small crawfish as do walleye.

Insects are not always the most nutritious food for game fish but insects such as flies, grasshoppers, butterflies, and caterpillars often make an attractive meal.

Leeches are great food for nearly every species of sport fish especially largemouth and smallmouth bass, walleye, northern pike, and even pan fish.

Hellgrammites are the aquatic larva of the dobsonfly. They tend to hide under rocks and are sought after by bass and trout.

Clams and mussels are often food for game fish, especially catfish.

The most popular and most nutritious food source for most game fish are other fish, which I will define here simply as bait fish. The reason bait fish are so important to game fish growth is they are readily available in most waters and they carry a high protein value. Bait fish will have the same nutrition value as the game fish in any specific water body since they get much of their nutrition from the water. In any given body of water, if the water contains a good nutrition mix, it will contain bait fish that are eating a well balanced diet. In these waters there will be plentiful bait fish and most likely larger game fish. A well balanced and nutritious diet will produce healthier fish which in turn will result in a much more productive spawn and the hatch of greater quantities of fry fish.

Since I have chosen to use the term bait fish to describe this food source, I should also explain the difference between bait fish and forage fish to avoid any confusion. Forage fish are any small fish that are preyed on in the wild by larger predator fish for food. The predators can be other larger fish of even birds and marine mammals. Bait fish, by contrast, are fish that are caught by anglers to use as bait for other fish. These two terms are overlapping since most bait fish are also forage fish and most forage fish are also bait fish, so let's just say they are the same.

There are more than 150 different types of freshwater bait or forage fish. Some of the more common are the skipjack herring, gizzard and threadfin shad, sunfish, goldfish, fathead minnow, golden shiner, various types of dace and chubs, suckers, smelt, alewives and many more. Some species of bait fish spawn many times each year and produce large quantities of offspring. The flathead minnow as an example spawns throughout the summer producing between 4000 and 5000 eggs each time.

Small forage or bait fish are very susceptible to water temperature. During periods of exceptional cold weather, it is not unusual to have large fish kills of these small fish. Although these fish kills do serious damage to the food base for the larger fish, the compensating factor is that they also breed and hatch new fry several times each year, replenishing the supply that was killed off.

One food source that is worth mentioning is the Alewife. Alewives are considered an invasive aquatic nuisance species and are not considered as a positive addition to any freshwater facility. Alewives are part of the herring family. Alewives are native to the Atlantic Ocean. Each spring the adult alewives migrate into fresh water to spawn. The young hatch in the rivers and then migrate back out to sea in the early fall. Alewives can survive in fresh water and many states have reported that the species has become established in many landlocked lakes.

Alewives can reproduce in fresh water. They reproduce rapidly and can become the dominant fish species in a freshwater lake. They are very efficient feeders and consume large quantities of zooplankton, which other species depend on as a food source. They are also known to eat large quantities of the small fry of other game fish. As a result, other small fish species suffer and often disappear from these waters. Alewife populations are known to go through fluctuating cycles, with annual die-offs of tens of thousands of fish at one time. The remaining fish however quickly re-build the population.

The alewife is a good example of how anglers can damage a water body by purchasing bait fish such as alewives and then dumping the remaining fish into a lake when their fishing is complete. This practice will quickly contaminate a facility with fish that are not considered beneficial to the food supply for the predator fish. Most species of game fish like to eat alewives so their existence in a lake or river is a double edged sword for the future of growing large fish in those waters.

Competition for Food

The population density, or the number of fish in a particular water body, is one of the most important factors in determining the growth rate of the fish in those waters. Assuming that a given water facility contains a certain quantity of forage fish and other food sources, it becomes obvious that the larger the number of predator fish that habitate those waters, the more competition that exists for that food. The term "stunted population" has been assigned to species of fish that are in high density, slow growing situations. This essentially means that there is sufficient food for the fish to survive, but not sufficient food to maintain growth throughout the life of the fish. One South Dakota study of yellow perch showed that one high density facility produced perch 4 years old that were about 5 inches long and weighed 0.3 pounds. The same species of fish with similar weather conditions and surroundings, in a low density situation grew to 10 inches and weighed more than 0.6 pounds in 4 years. That's a growth factor of 2 to 1, which is very significant.

When density is low, food is more abundant and growth rates are substantially faster. These same studies showed that perch populations of 50 to 60 pounds per acre of water produced slow growth rates and a population of 10 to 20 pounds per acre produced fast growth rates. A similar study of largemouth bass in idwestern waters showed 60 to 100 pounds per acre, which is fairly common in the Midwest, produced slow growing bass but populations of 10 to 20 pounds per acre produced fast growth rates for bass. Some typical variations of 5 year old fish in different population situations are shown on the chart below.

Length variations (inches) for 5 year old fish, related to population density			
Fish Species	**High Density**	**Average Density**	**Low Density**
Bluegill	5.3	6.8	8.2
Channel Cat	10.7	13.4	17.5
Largemouth Bass	12.0	15.2	18.2
Smallmouth Bass	10.4	13.3	16.5
Walleye	13.3	18.7	23.1
Yellow perch	7.0	8.8	10.7

It is significant to note that the growth is nearly 50% greater for fish that are in low density waters than it is for fish in high density situations.

There is another aspect of this growth variation that might be significant in some waters. Slower growing fish species tend to live longer than those in the faster growing category.

Fishing Pressure

It is fitting that I leave this area for the last on this subject, because it is also the most interesting. It is controversial among scientists and perhaps more so among anglers. For years we felt that fish are fish, and every time you put food in front of them they will want to eat it. I personally have never felt that way and over the years I have developed a policy of not fishing the same area two days in a row, and typically I will wait three days before returning to an area to fish. I dealt with this subject in some detail in one of my books titled "Freshwater Fighters." At that time I was coming at the subject from another angle, namely, how often will a fish come back to bite once it has been caught. In those studies I got sidetracked by work being done by PETA, an organization that was lobbying to outlaw fishing because they maintained that hooking a fish caused that fish great pain. The studies they were using as the basis of their argument contained serious flaws. They were neglecting the fact that the reduced size of the brain of a fish indicates that a fish has no central cortex in its brain. It is the central cortex that processes all information received from nerve endings and tells the brain that pain is being inflicted. Without a central cortex, it is considered impossible for a fish to feel pain as we understand it. Trauma, on the other hand, is a condition that if repeated might eventually create a memory in the brain of a fish. As an example, if a fish is caught and allowed to drop on the floor of a boat and bounce around for a long period of time, might remember that traumatic experience if it were to happen again in a short enough period of time. If that fish is caught repeatedly, it might soon realize that attacking a lure or bait, thinking it was food, causes it serious trauma and it will start getting hesitant to strike out the next time. There are an increasing number of studies that are proving this to be true.

A very thorough study was conducted over a four year period by the University of Calgary in Canada. The study showed rather conclusively that fish caught over and over eventually develop a "hook resistance." This means that the trauma of being caught, spending minutes out of the water, being slammed around in a boat, man-handled for hook removal then thrown back into the water, eventually makes that fish hesitant to come back and bite again. The Canadian study results showed that the catch rate from four similar lakes that were heavily fished with a catch and release policy, was four times less that the catch rate of another four similar lakes that were lightly fished.

Since most areas in Canada were moving toward a complete catch and release policy, these results sent shock waves through the Canadian wildlife system. Since many of the Canadian Provinces derive a great deal of revenue from visiting anglers, a healthy fishing environment is important to the nation's economy. The study also showed that the fish were noticeably smaller in the lakes that were heavily fished. This would not be surprising if a fish begins to hesitate to strike out after bait, it will eventually eat less and its growth rate will be stunted.

In Fisherman Magazine recently published a short article about the possibility that catch and release practices are affecting the growth rate of bass. The article was based on a study from a relatively small lake in Michigan conducted by The University of Wisconsin. The data was derived from electro-fishing results and records of tagged fish that were caught by anglers in a controlled fishing environment. Barbless hooks were used by the anglers that participated in the study and the time that the fish were kept out of the water was kept to a minimum. The results of this study are illustrated below. I re-constructed the chart for my convenience, but the results were not altered.

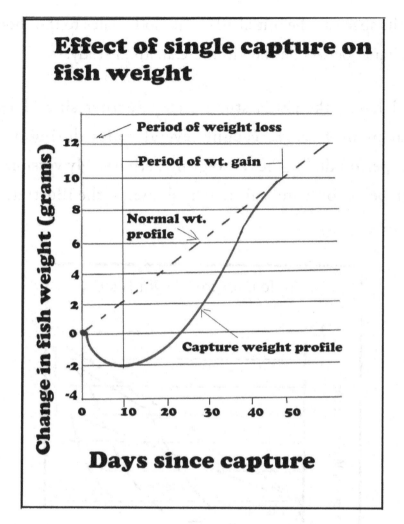

Effect of single capture on fish weight

Change in fish weight (grams)

Period of weight loss

Period of wt. gain

Normal wt. profile

Capture weight profile

Days since capture

This chart indicates that a bass caught only once, goes through a weight loss for the first 10 days after being returned to the water. After the initial 10 day period, the fish begins to eat actively again and begins to gain back the weight previously lost. Eventually, between 30 and 40 days after capture, the fish is back on the normal growth path for its species. The initial 10 day period relates to the "hook hesitant" period defined in the Canadian study.

I have taken this study a step further since I feel that many fish are caught several times during a 10 day period during heavy angling activity. My version of fish behavior using this data is shown in the illustration below.

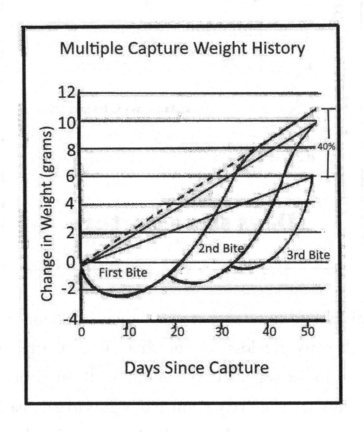

I have not altered the first bite data, but I take it a step further. At the ten day period after the first bite, the fish begins to feed actively to regain lost weight. Because of its active feeding, the fish is hooked again during this feeding period. This second bite and catch triggers the same reaction as the first bite, the fish becomes hesitant for another ten days, then starts to feed again, but because it never regained all of its initial weight, it takes the fish longer to regain the weight and it never reaches the normal growth curve.

During the heavy feeding after the second bite (ten days later), the fish is caught again from a third bite and the same process is repeated. This time the eventual stabilization weight is even lower than after the second bite. If I now draw the growth curve through the fifty day mark, it indicates that the growth rate could be as much as 40% lower. If this pattern continues, this fish will eventually be less healthy from eating less and smaller than its normal growth rate. This type of behavior would tend to validate the results of the Canadian study. The numbers here are not exact but the trend is obvious. The more often a fish is caught, the less healthy it becomes.

There are other reputable studies that show similar size reduction statistics. Both of these studies were conducted on waters that were well known for catching big catfish. The Santee Cooper lakes in South Carolina have been known for many years as the place to go in the south for big catfish. I found data provided by wildlife officials that shows that the catfish size in these waters has been shrinking steadily for over ten years as illustrated in the chart shown below.

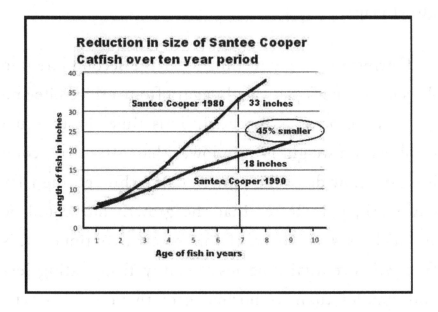

The catfish size reduction over the ten year period was 45% which is an alarming reduction in size.

Another popular eastern river known for large catfish is the James River in Virginia. Similar studies conducted by the state revealed that the catfish in this river are also getting smaller as illustrated below.

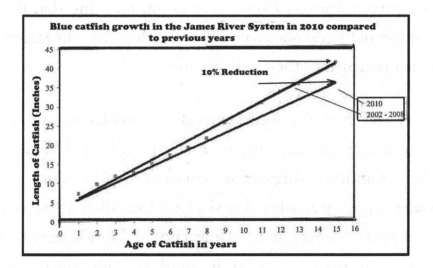

This data shows a reduction in fish size of 10% over a period of two years. A continuation of this trend will put the James River in the same category as Santee Cooper over a ten year period. These size reductions are very significant.

I have become convinced that heavy fishing pressure is causing fish health to become effected, resulting in fewer and smaller fish being caught. One cause of this phenomenon is the scheduling of too many fishing tournaments over too short a period of time. There are some lakes and rivers where tournaments are scheduled nearly every day of the week during prime fishing periods. Aside from the problem of smaller and less healthy fish, there has been some published information that indicates that in some of the less controlled tournaments, there is a mortality rate of between 3% and 7% on each event, meaning that this number of fish do not survive the trauma of the tournament when returned to their native waters.

If you carefully read some of the articles written by tournament participants, normally professional anglers, there is an increasing dialog about bass depletion in some waters. A recent article written by Dr. Mike Allen, a professor of aquatic sciences at the University of Florida, revealed that many anglers who fish in multi day tournaments are complaining that the availability of bass during the later days of these tournaments is dropping significantly. The implication here is that the number of catchable fish is much lower during the later days of a long tournament. Tournament officials quickly respond to these complaints by indicating that the complaining anglers are the ones who are not surviving through the last days of a tournament. These same officials put aside the theory that the fish that are caught and returned to the water during the early days of the tournament are just not coming back to bite during the later days because of the "hook avoidance" theory.

Competition officials also point out that major tournaments are only held on lakes where there is a very high population of bass. On average, competition lakes have about 12 bass per acre and often as high as 20 fish per acre. A typical competition lake would contain from 200,000 up to 500,000 bass. In an average tournament only about 0.2 percent of the resident fish will be weighed in which represents a very small percentage of the total bass available.

Of course this explanation leaves out the fact that a relatively small percentage of resident fish are actually vulnerable to being caught in any lake. Tagging studies have shown that between 10 and 40 pecent of the bass in any lake are actually caught each year. Reduce this number by the increasing number of local and minor tournaments that are held on a lake each year and it suddenly begins to look like the complaints may have some merit.

With all of this information in hand, what can the average angler do to start **Fishing Different** to help solve this problem. There are some obvious things that can be done. Practice good conservation habits with the fish and the waters in which they live. Try not to return to the same fishing spot day after day, take breaks of at least two days in any specific spot. Follow the activities of your fishery agencies, both local, state, and federal. Participate in activities that relate to fishing habitat. Work with local youth groups that sponsor fishing activities to help the next generations become conscious of good angling practices. Carry a bottle of citric soft drink in your boat, if your fish bleeds when you remove the hook, spill some of this liquid into the area effected to help the healing process. If you are not going to photograph your catch, try to remove the hook while the fish is still in the water assuming of course that you can do it safely. Don't force your fish retrievals. Take the fish in slowly but steadily, if the fish wants to run, let it take drag, when it's finished running, start your retrieval. Always check your drag to insure that it is set to permit your fish to run. If you practice these simple things, you will be doing your part by **Fishing Different.**

Chapter Six

Sonar's Valuable Contribution to Successful Fishing

"Anyone who stops learning is old, whether at twenty or eighty. Anyone who keeps learning stays young. The greatest thing in life is keep your mind young."

Henry Ford

The history of many of our country's heroes and the battles they fought to retain our freedom is often lost to the younger generations. Many of the benefits of technology that we take for granted today, were established and developed under the great hardship of wars previously fought. Fish finding sonar technology is but one of those benefits. It is my opinion that a good understanding of this equipment is **THE MOST IMPORTANT** knowledge when an angler needs to improve technique or catch rate.

It was early May, 1942 on the submarine USS Wahoo that was operating in very dangerous waters of the Sea of Japan.

Captain Dudley "Mush" Morton was leaning over the shoulder of his 19 year old sonar operator Jeff Mahoney. Mahoney had enlisted shortly after the war began and was sent to sea on the Wahoo with a total of three months specialized training as a sonar operator. The Wahoo was running silent in search of its next target. Mahoney was staring intently at his sonar screen which was a simple scanning sweep beam. More important he was listening to the pinging sounds in his headset, the sounds of an approaching Japanese ship. This was a critical time and Mahoney was the critical part of this crude system since he provided interpretation of these strange beeping sounds. He would periodically signal to the Captain with hand signals the distance from the approaching ship in thousands of meters and quietly whisper to the Captain the approaching ship's course in degrees.

The closer the target ship approached, the higher the tension became for all of the crew of 83 sailors and officers aboard the Wahoo. When the Captain was certain that he had a kill shot, he instructed the crew to fire both torpedoes at the incoming Japanese ship. Moments later the crew broke its silence with a cheer after the sounds of the exploding ship rattled the submarine.

Unfortunately, despite the successes of this crude sonar equipment, the US Navy lost 52 submarines and more than

1500 crewmen during WWII. Among those losses was the USS Wahoo. It was sunk exiting the Sea of Japan after sinking 4 ships. The USS Wahoo had sunk more than 60,000 tons of Japanese ships during its active tours and ranks among the submarines with the highest kill rates of the war.

This story not only illustrates the heroism of the young men that manned these submarines, but is also an indication of how far sonar technology has come, not only for wartime use but also as a key part of today's fishing support equipment. It has been more than 70 years since those first critical uses of sonar and it took about 40 of those years for sonar equipment to find its way effectively into the sport of fishing as standard equipment.

The name sonar evolved from the terms SOund NAvigation and Ranging which simply means that this technology, based on the use of sound, is used for navigation and determining the range of a target. Sonar is based on the principles of sound wave reflection. Like electricity, sound waves can travel over long distances. Unlike electricity, however, sound decays with the distance it travels and the angular position taken from the direction of the sound origin. As an example, if you are sitting in a theatre, the best position for hearing the best quality sound is directly in front of the sound source. Similarly the further back you sit from the sound source, the poorer is the sound quality. The further sideways from the sound source you move, the lower the quality of the sound. For this reason, many theatres have installed well planned amplifying systems so every seat has good quality sound.

Fish finding sonar systems do not have the benefit of these complicated amplifying systems. They simply transmit sound waves directly down into the water. If the sound wave hits an object the signal is reflected back to the transmitting source. This reflected signal is sent to a small computer which interprets the signal, and displays an image on a small screen. Imagine yourself in a large room with nothing on the walls or floor. If you shout, that shout will return to your ears as an echo, having been bounced off the walls and floor and returned to your ears a few seconds after you shouted. The time delay of that echo will depend on the size of the room and your distance from the walls that reflected the sound. In that situation you are in fact acting as a piece of sonar equipment. Your mouth is the signal transmitter, your brain is the computer and your ears are the display mechanism. If you now start placing objects around this room and again you shout, the return echo will be much weaker because the objects that were added have absorbed some of the sound. This is the same principle that is used to create sonar images. If the sound waves hit a fish, a small portion will be absorbed and the remaining signal will be reflected back to the processor in the unit. The small computer in a sonar unit converts these signal changes into images that are projected on the sonar screen.

A fish finding sonar, mounted on a boat, transmits signals down into the water, but these signals are continuously transmitted thousands of times each second. Even though the signals are transmitted straight downward, they also can be detected at some angle sideways to the transmitted source, but the further away from the straight downward angle, the lower the transmitted power. Most sonar used for fishing equipment uses an angle of 10 degrees away from center to be the maximum angle at which a useable sound signal can be received. At angles greater than 10 degrees, there is still a detectable signal but it is not considered useful for detection purposed because the power level at those angles is too low. In technical terms, the power level at 10 degrees either side of straight down is defined as the half power point also called the minus -3 db point. This theory is illustrated in the diagram below. More recent improvements in this technology now permit wider angles to be used but the standard is still a composite of 20 degrees.

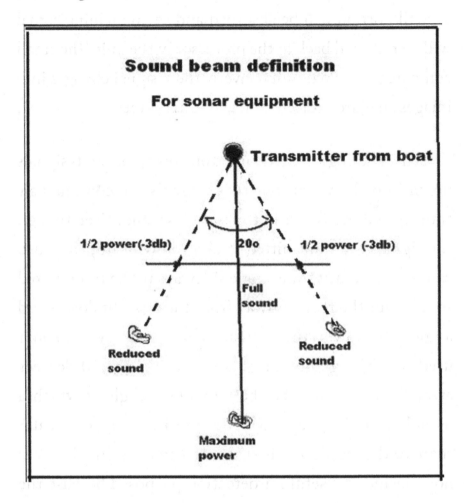

This illustration shows a two dimensional sonar beam running 10 degrees either side of center or a 20 degrees angle, boundary to boundary. In fact the beam is transmitted thousands of times a second and emits in all directions, so the area of coverage below the boat is actually better represented by a cone of transmitted signals as shown below.

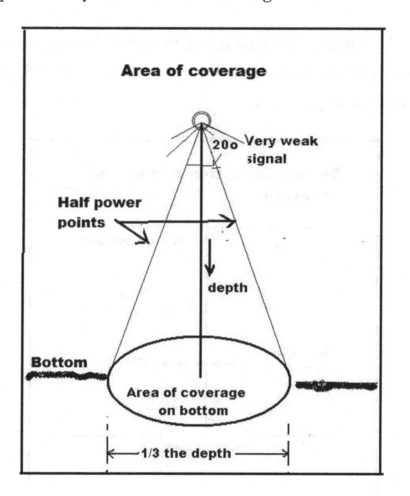

This illustrates that coverage depicted on your Sonar screen is a cone extending downward to the bottom. The diameter of the circular area shown on the bottom is approximately one third of the depth of the water so that in 30 feet of water the area of coverage shown on the screen would represent a diameter of about ten feet on the bottom. These numbers result from simple geometry.

As a fish swims through the cone of the transmitted signals below the boat, its image is created on the display screen as shown below.

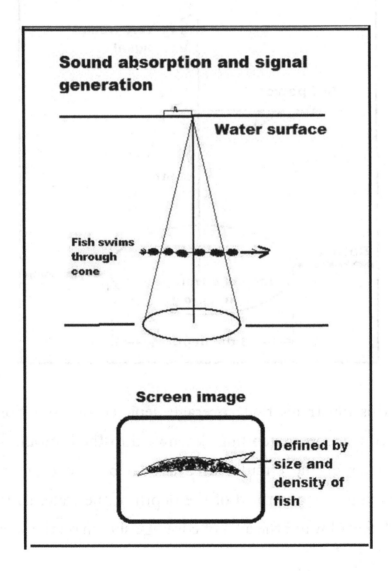

Sound absorption and signal generation

Water surface

Fish swims through cone

Screen image

Defined by size and density of fish

The reason the signal of the fish is shown as an arch is due to two factors. First the power of the signal hitting the fish is greatest when the signal is transmitted straight down or the fish is right in the middle of the cone of transmission. Secondly, the signal gets slightly weaker as the fish transitions through the cone so there is less of a reflected signal sent to the computer when the fish nears the outside boundary of the cone. It should be noted that the only time a fish signal is a perfect arch, is when the fish swims directly through the center of the cone. Most sonar instruction manuals will have you believe that all fish images are perfect arches when in fact most are not. Because of the power and distance relationships, the closer to the surface the fish passes through the signal, the steeper the arch will be, the deeper from the surface the fish is located, the flatter the arch will be. In very deep water, like 60 to 100 feet, the fish image might be a nearly straight line. Also the longer the fish stays in the cone, the longer the arch or line will be. The concept of depth is shown in the illustration below.

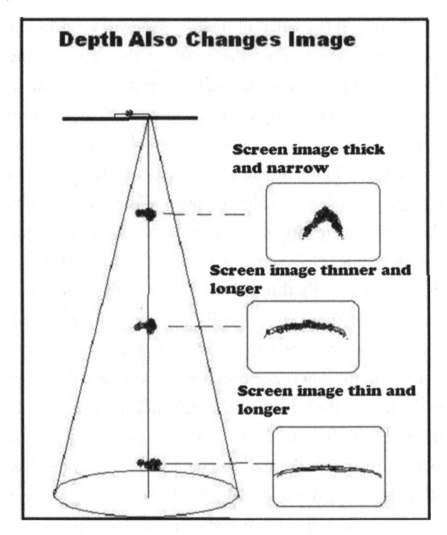

Depth Also Changes Image

Screen image thick and narrow

Screen image thnner and longer

Screen image thin and longer

There are a couple of situations that need further explanation. There must be motion between the boat and the fish in order for an arch to be generated. If the boat is not moving forward and a fish sits still in the cone, the image will only be a dot on the screen. Also if the boat is moving and a fish is swimming along in the cone at the same speed and direction as the boat, which happens fairly often, the signal will appear as a straight line across the screen.

There is a very important aspect of sonar signal processing that should be understood to get the maximum amount of information from the sonar system. The strength of the return signal that is reflected off of a fish is a function of the mass of the body of the fish. In other words, the bigger and fatter the fish, the more mass its body will have. This will be indicated by the thickness of the image that is displayed on the screen. In color display units, this will probably show up as a different color at the center of the arch. In a non-color unit, it may show as a grey area in the middle of the arch. If you have your own sonar unit and you keep the unit set at the same settings all of the time, you will eventually be able to estimate the size of the fish that you are seeing by the thickness and color of the center of the image. The length of the arch image has nothing to do with the size of the fish: it only reflects the time that the fish has remained in the signal cone. The thicker the arch is at its center, the bigger the fish actually is.

There are many occasions when an image, other than a complete arch, appears on the screen. As an example, if a fish passes through the cone but only passes through a side portion, the fish image will appear as a slanted line or an half arch. Many anglers get confused thinking that these half arches or slanted lines are not fish. Actually it is rare that the screen image actually looks like a complete arch.

A question that has been asked many times is how to set the various setting available, like sensitivity, tone etc. The best settings for any sonar unit are those that were made at the factory. If you decide to play with your settings, your equipment manual should tell you how to return to your factory settings. When you find them, leave them alone. The only element that you might adjust is the sensitivity. This adjustment can sometimes clear up water that is otherwise cloudy or contains debris. I also have found that I never use the zoom adjustments. I have developed a large file of image photos with the zoom set at zero. If I adjust the zoom upward, it only makes the images larger and it is impossible to make a determination of size from the expanded image. If you use a zoom setting, use it all the time. Some anglers who are experienced with their equipment and regularly make setting changes recommend that these changes be made at a time when fish or structure is being displayed so that you can immediately see the effects of the changes that are being made.

Sonar capability in fish finders has progressed a long way since the first "little green box" introduced by Lowrance in 1959. Over in the last ten years, technology has advanced so much that significant improvements had been added to standard sonar equipment.

The first recent upgrade was the addition of down imaging and side imaging. These changes permitted the angler to look out beyond the limitations of the early units, viewing bottom features and structures that were ten times the distance of the earlier units. Looking out hundreds of feet beyond a boat allowed anglers to view structures and bottom features that were missed with the simpler sonar that viewed only areas near or under the boat. Side scan technology permitted this capability. Down imaging arrived at the same time permitting much clearer definition of structures being viewed. Bushes and trees actually looked like bushes and trees when viewed with down imaging systems.

When these two new technologies were added to conventional sonar, there were two negative factors that kept many anglers from moving up to the new systems. The first negative was the cost. Costs to gain all the new advantages were nearly five times the cost of conventional units. The second negative involved the angler. There was so much information presented for viewing that to gain advantage of the technology the angler had to thoroughly understand and interpret what was being viewed. In some cases it took three or four separate images on the screen to fully understand what was shown.

In a fairly short period some of these negatives were removed. The cost of gaining down- and side-scan imaging came way down to the point where a sonar including all of these features could be purchased for a price nearly as low as the conventional systems when they were first introduced.

More recently even better features have been added. A feature called CHIRP (Compressed High Intensity Radar Pulse) is now available in some systems. This technology has been available in military applications for several years but has now found its way into commercially available equipment. Original systems sent a single frequency pulse down into the water. The CHIRP technology sends a varying frequency signal on top of the original pulse to provide the image viewer a much better definition of the image being displayed.

CHIRP has been defined as a technology that equates to the difference between conventional television and high definition television. Another comparison that will be appreciated by my older readers is the difference between radio signals before frequency modulation (FM) was discovered: no more static. Users of CHIRP systems claim that it provides a degree of target separation where bait schools can be better defined, perhaps even permitting the identification of the bait species.

My concern about all of these new capabilities is the ability of the average angler to understand what is being displayed. I fear that using all of this new capability will take much of the fun from the sport, especially from the equipment operator. Professional anglers will, of course, continue to endorse these changes because they need to spend less time looking around for fish and therefore will have more time available for catching the fish. For the every-day angler however, I fear that there is so much information available to them that they will begin missing the real important images. Fishing will become confusing rather than an enjoyment for the average angler.

Based on my personal experience with the hundreds of anglers who attend my lectures each year, we are still in a period of learning where the majority of the "average anglers" do not yet completely understand how to interpret what they are viewing on their conventional sonar screens. This is not because these anglers have any learning deficiency but simply because they do not get to spend as much time on the water fishing as is required to thoroughly understand the common sonar images that get repeated over and over, day after day. Once an angler has reached an appropriate level of skill interpreting common Sonar images, it will be time to start **Fishing Different** by moving up to the more complex sonar systems.

To help develop a better understanding of common sonar screen images, I have presented several of these images in the next chapter.

CHAPTER SEVEN

Interpreting and Understanding Sonar Images

"Make everything as simple as possible, but not simpler."

Albert Einstein

I believe nearly every angler that is serious about improving technique and catch rate will fish from a boat with some form of sonar equipment installed. What I am finding, however, is that many anglers have not taken the time to truly understand the meaning of what they are observing on their sonar screens. Sonar technology is perhaps the most important invention available to today's anglers. There is little doubt in my mind that this equipment has doubled or even tripled the quantity and quality of fish being caught in fresh water in the last two decades.

To some, technology of this type may appear too complex to enhance their fishing enjoyment. In this chapter I will try to simplify the part of sonar that gets right to the heart of the equipment's value. As Einstein suggests, I will try not to make it sound so simple that it loses its appeal. The sonar equipment itself does all of the real work, but understanding the images that are displayed is the task of the angler and if not properly understood, sonar will be of little or no value for improving catch rates. I'm going to try and present some of the most basic images here to help with the understanding of how this amazing instrument can help every angler improve techniques and results. I will show images from conventional, single image sonar rather than complicating the discussion with down and side scan imaging.

I mentioned in the previous chapter that most sonar units when shipped from the factory have been set in such a way as to present the best overall quality of the display. Sometimes there is one exception to this rule and it involves the setting of the fish ID and the fish alarm. I have always recommended that the fish ID and fish alarm be turned OFF. The beeping noise that accompanies the fish ID and alarm is annoying and distracting and is often triggered by items floating in the water that ARE not fish. I also believe that the raw image displayed with the alarm on is less informative than when the alarm ID turned off. The composite image shown below illustrates that.

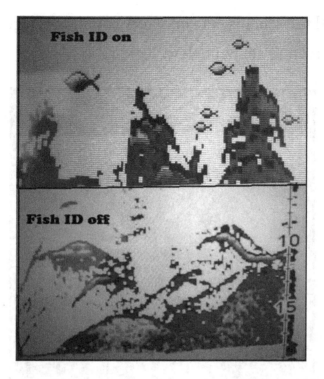

The lower illustration is a more realistic picture of two brush piles surrounded by small bait fish and several predator fish. It shows the feeding activity represented by the changing depth of the predator fish which does not show in the upper segment of the illustration. Both images do indicate the presence of fish but the lower image is a more realistic indication of fish activity.

Bait fish activity is key for attracting large predator fish. If you locate bait fish schools, the big fish that you are after will not be far behind. One of the more common types of bait fish are shad. Most southern waters are filled with shad and the schools take on a very common image on your sonar screen as shown below.

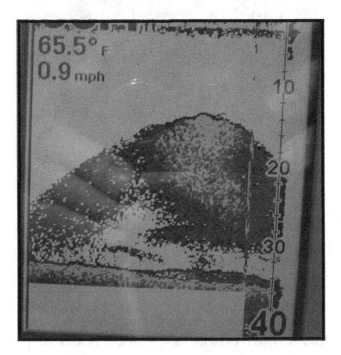

An image of this density might represent a school of four to five thousand small shad. Shad schools always have a heavy center core of fish that are packed together for security. Shad images will almost always have a "tail like" fall off of fish on each side of the central core. Predators will always attack the seemingly weaker fish in these "tails" or they will attach the top edges of the school as shown below.

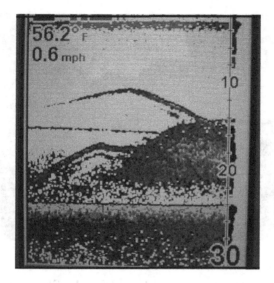

The fish swimming in the tails and edges of these large schools appear to the predators as weak or wounded fish that cannot keep up with the movement of the main school.

Another common bait fish is the herring or alewife. These small fish like the colder water and will always be found near the bottom and in areas where springs feed the water body. Massive schools of herring often fool the casual image observer because they look much like a false bottom as shown in the image below.

This image shows a massive school of herring nearly ten feet thick. Again here the predator fish shown will always attack the herring from the top side.

While we are discussing cold water entering a water body from underground springs, it is possible to locate these springs with sonar. A common sonar image of a spring is shown below.

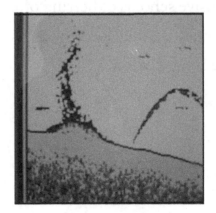

In most cases the first indication of a spring is a mound of silt or sand on the bottom accompanied by a series of small dots seeming to rise to the surface. Water usually enters at a temperature of around 50 degrees. As this cold water is warmed by the surrounding water it rises toward the surface. This is clearly shown in this image. It might be noted that this image also shows a fish nearby. Fish will tend to seek out these springs for the cooler water especially in the heat of the summer.

In waters where perch are located, the schools of small perch are easily recognized as shown below.

The small perch will form schools that when undisturbed appear as small balls located at any level of the water column. Larger perch ranging in size from 3 to 12 inches will appear as shown below.

For the larger perch, the actual density of the larger body makes the fish individually visible.

Catfish are easily recognized due to the thickness of their body. Catfish at rest close to the bottom are often mistaken for a log. The distinguishing element that identifies it as a fish is the space between the fish image and the bottom as shown below.

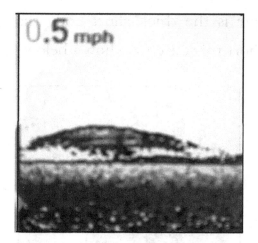

Stripers usually are visible in schools and often the smaller schools are represented by overlapping arches as shown below.

Crappie are usually found in small groups and normally are near structure, but sometimes are visible without structure as shown below. The feature that identifies the fish as crappie is the thick short body that provides an image of a short thick arch as shown below.

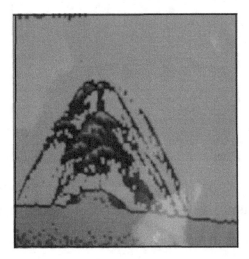

Bass are the prize for many anglers and bass are often seen in schools as shown below.

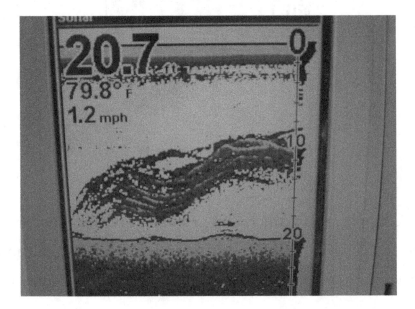

Feeding bass usually are seen moving up and down in the water column as shown.

I mentioned earlier that bait fish often take shelter along drop offs which makes them vulnerable to predators as shown below.

In the warmer summer months fish will often suspend in deeper water at a particular depth. A group of suspended fish is shown below.

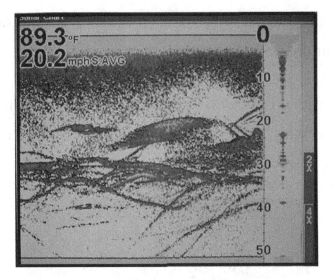

I make mention of jigging in several places in this book. Anglers can identify the location of their vertical jig by moving the jig close to the sonar sensor and viewing the up and down movement of the jig as shown below.

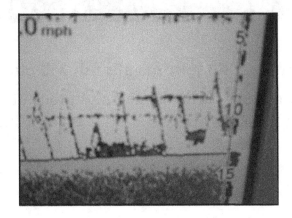

Brush piles and rock piles will draw fish as shown below.

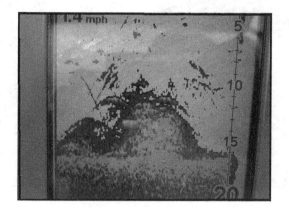

Rock Piles offer the same attraction.

As a fitting ending to these common sonar images, every angler wishes to see a large school of large bass attacking a small school of shad as shown below.

The sonar illustrations that I have included here are but a few that I consider somewhat standard in a freshwater facility. These are the images that are easy to understand but every image on an angler's sonar screen tells a story of what is going on beneath the surface. These images, if properly used to change an anglers fishing procedures, will most certainly increase the catch rate and aid every anglers desire to begin **fishing different.**

······································

Chapter Eight

Fishing Depth and Distance, a Key to Success

······································

"Any fool can know. The point is to understand."

Albert Einstein

We have discussed several issues relative to the water condition and fish behavior. One subject that demands attention is the correct depth to fish under different conditions. There is no mystical guesswork here and I am not aware of any myths that we have been following that need clarification. It's just that many anglers haven't taken the time to understand why they are fishing right where the fish are located and they can't get a bite. We know that fish will seek the most comfortable depth based on water temperature but an angler may not always know exactly what that depth is under different conditions. Also seeking fish around docks and other near-shore structure where the angler is casting lures or other types of bait, the depth is not quite as important as it is where fish may be suspended in deeper water or feeding actively where they will be changing their depth based on their search for food.

We discussed earlier the effect of bright sunlight on fish. Their eyes are close to the top of their head so their natural field of view is outward and upward. To look downward a fish would have to move its body for better eye position, so looking downward is not the normal field of view for most fish. The result of this physical characteristic is that the best way to attract a fish to your bait or lure is to make sure that it is moved at or above the position of the fish. The previous chapter showed several sonar images of different fish in different situations. Those images normally tell the angler exactly where to place the bait or lure. The illustration below is another sonar image of a school of bass that are searching for food. When bass are packed together like this they are always in search of a big school of bait.

The school in this photo is in 36 feet of water and the center of the school at the time of this image is located at a depth of about 20 feet. If you were in a position to cast toward this school of fish you would use a lure that would get you to between 10 and 13 feet of depth. This would put your lure just above the top of the fish. If you were trolling you would want your bait at that same general depth. Since these fish are feeding they will move up and down in the water column. Keeping the lure at 13 feet will still keep the bait slightly above the eye level of most of the fish and well within their strike zone. Seeing an image like this with so many hungry fish is an anglers dream. If you get your bait anywhere near the suggested depth, you will almost certainly get a strike. If you are trolling you probably will get multiple hits at the same time.

If you were casting a lure or other bait around structure such as a dock, you would probably be looking to attract the attention of one or two bass rather than a complete school as shown above. Most anglers that fish around shoreline structure use lures that they can finesse to different depths, like jigs tipped with plastic worms. These baits are normally cast at the surface and will slowly sink as the angler moves the rod tip to make the jig head move. Most of the time if there is a bass in the general area it will strike at the bait as it sinks and before it reached the bottom. If a bass sees a bait dropping, it will swim down to catch it, but this is one of the few times when a fish will go down to strike out at bait.

Now the question is, "How do you know the depth your bait is at when you are using live bait or trolling with artificial lures?" With live bait it is not too difficult to put your bait where you want it if you understand a few basic concepts. A simple illustration of your boat moving through the water is shown below.

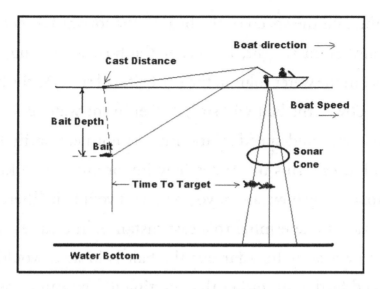

There are several factors this illustration highlights. The first is that your sonar sensor is pointing straight downward with its signal forming a cone as described in Chapter Six. This means when you see fish on the sonar screen, they are located below the boat, within the cone of the sonar scan. (Remember the diameter of the sonar cone on the bottom is approximately ⅓the depth of the water). Remember, when your boat is moving, your bait is far behind the boat and it will take some time for it to reach the point where you first saw the fish.

Exactly where your bait is located is a function of four things: the distance behind the boat where your bait was originally placed, which I will call the "Cast Distance;" the weight of the rig including the sinker weight; the bait weight; and the speed of the boat in the forward direction. For any given weight, the faster the boat is moving, the higher in the water column the live bait will ride. As the boat slows down, the bait will sink deeper in the water column. (This depth and speed relationship is not necessarily true for all lures.) This illustrates how important it is to know approximately how far out you have cast your bait. There are two ways to determine this cast distance. The easiest way to know exactly how far out the bait is located would be to hand feed it out rather than casting it. You can measure the line out 12 inches at a time until you reach the desired distance. This method is fairly precise and will allow you to put several lines out at different distances and still know how far from the boat they are. Most anglers, however, do not want to take the time to hand feed their line.

Another way to determine the cast distance is to take a few minutes before you go fishing and make a few practice casts on land. Measure and record your cast distances for these casts. This gives you a general idea of how far you throw the bait when you cast it from the boat. Once you determine your average cast, you can vary that by throwing harder or softer. This method is not precise but it is normally close enough. I believe that once you know your normal cast distance, it will not vary too much each time you go out fishing. A few minutes at the start of the season measuring your distance will pay dividends as you increase your fishing activity.

The other information that you need to know is the approximate weight of your rig. This weight will include the actual bait, the swivels and the sinker weight. I have found that a 1/4 ounce bullet weight on a Carolina rig produces about a 3/8 ounce total weight when using medium sized live bait. The weight of the live bait is nearly negligible because of its neutral buoyancy.

The last influencing factor is your boat speed. As I said, the faster the boat goes, the higher the bait will flow in the water column. If your equipment includes a GPS, you will have a visual indication of your actual speed through the water and this will be fairly precise. If you do not have a GPS, you can use a small portable hand held GPS, which is very adequate to determine boat speed. I can't over emphasize the importance of knowing and controlling your boat speed, when trolling, the speed of the boat is a very important factor. Live bait flows best through the water at speeds around 0.5 MPH. or even slightly slower. Most main boat motors will not troll down to this low speed so trolling at these slow speeds will usually require the use of a trolling motor or some other method of controlled drifting. If you increase you boat speed above about 1.0 MPH, the live bait will tend to tumble or roll in the water and you will lose the natural movement of the bait. On the other hand, lures work best at speeds in excess of 2 MPH. For that reason I normally do not recommend trolling with combinations of both live baits and artificial lures. If you are not sure of your boat speed, you can hold your rod tip over the side of the boat and watch the lure or bait action. At the correct speed you will observe the bait or lure performing properly.

"OK," you might say, "I have all of that information, what do I do with it?" Well, I have made the rest of that challenge easy for you. I have made a series of tests with different weights and different boat speeds. I have constructed a series of charts which can be read directly, knowing your bait weight, cast distance and boat speed. These charts are shown below for three different cast distances, 50, 75 and 100 feet.

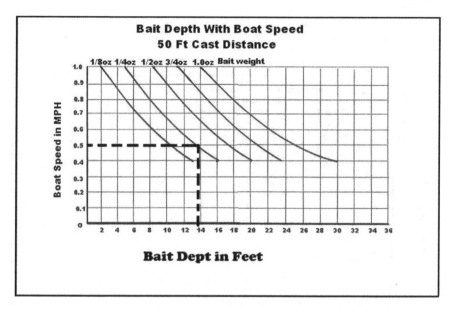

To find your bait depth you enter the chart at your boat speed, say 0.5 MPH and read over to your bait weight, in the example it would be ¼ ounce. At that point you read down to see the bait depth which is 14 feet. The same process is used for longer cast distances in the following charts.

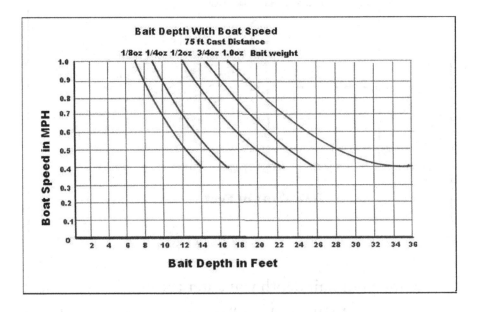

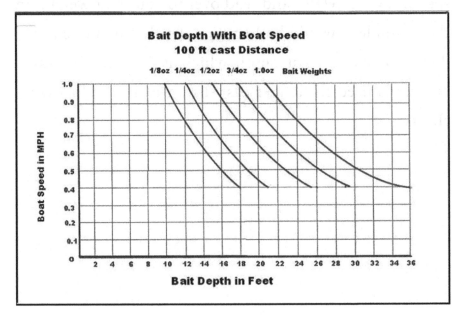

For seasonal fishing or for fishing a species that might be deeper in the water, I have also prepared these charts for 1 ounce and 2 ounce weights as shown below.

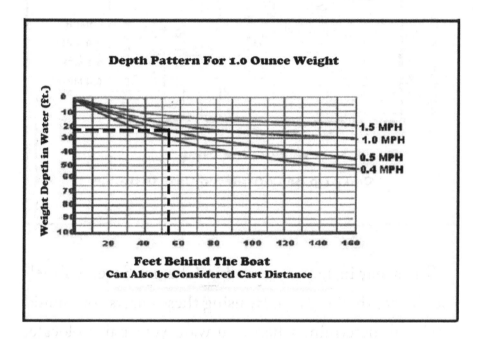

For the heavier weights you would enter the chart at your cast distance behind the boat and move up to your boat speed. Where those points intersect you move to the left and determine your bait or weight depth.

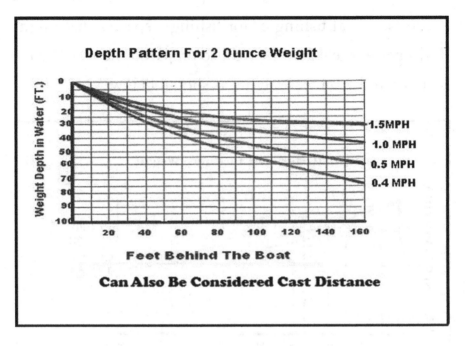

The sonar images discussed in Chapter Seven will tell you the depth of the fish. By using these charts you should be able to determine where you want your bait to locate, which will be at a depth that is slightly above the depth where the fish were located. If your bait is not where you want it, you can adjust the speed of the boat to bring the bait to the desired depth. Of course you can also read these charts in reverse, first picking your desired depth, moving up to the bait weight and reading the correct boat speed that will put you at that depth. These numbers will vary slightly because none of the values are ever constant or exact. The charts are, however, close enough that you will be able to get the bait where you want it for the best catch rate. If you plan on doing a lot of fishing, it would be advisable to take time to run your own test and re-plot these curves to match your fishing conditions. The line that you are using will affect the fishing depths of your rig or lure. The charts shown above were constructed from test data taken with 8 pound test monofilament line. Braided lines will be slightly heavier and you might want to add a couple of ounces to your rig weight estimates, to get the correct depth from the charts. When you are finished making all of the calculations from the charts but you have doubts about your desired depth, remember go a little faster to insure the bait is higher rather than lower in the water column.

Once you are rigged, baited, and your lines are in the water, the only real control you have over bait depth is your boat speed. When you see fish on your Sonar device, you might determine that at the speed you are at, the bait will be below the fish. If this is the case, simply increase the boat speed, raising the bait to the desired depth.

You will have time to make these adjustments in speed because it will take some time for your bait to reach the point where you first saw the fish. There is a simple equation that will permit you to calculate this time period as shown below.

$$\text{Time to target (seconds)} = \text{cast distance in feet} \div \text{boat speed in MPH} \times 1.46$$

"Come on," you say, "You don't expect me to make that calculation in my head while I'm fishing do you?" No, I do not, because I have made it easy for you by plotting another series of curves where you can simply look up the answer. This series of curves is shown below.

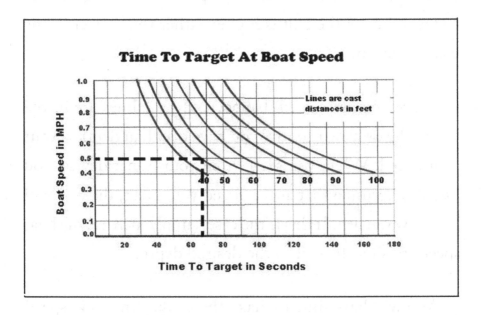

On this chart you simply look at your boat speed and enter the chart at that speed. Move over to the cast distance that you are using and where those two points intersect, you read the time that it will take for your bait to reach the target. In the example shown above, you enter at a boat speed of 0.5 MPH, move to the 50 foot cast distance and read your time to the target is about 68 seconds. With a little practice you will be able to tell your fishing partners when to expect a fish to bite and they will be amazed at your knowledge and expertise. An average angler with an average cast distance using a Carolina rig can normally expect the time to a strike to be about one minute.

Of course, I do not expect that you will remember all of this complicated stuff, but if you're a smart angler, you will make copies of these charts, or even cut them out of this book. Have them laminated and keep them in your boat for easy reference. I know with time and use, you will come to realize that this was the best move you've made to improve your catch rate.

I have been asked, "How does this work if I'm trolling with artificial lures?" With lures the whole game changes, but in some instances it is simpler. If you are using artificial lures and trolling, there is a good chance that you are using some form of crank bait. These baits have lips on the front end. These lips make the lure dive to a specific depth when trolled at their optimum speed. There is no way for you to determine what the optimum speed is for a specific lure, so I recommend that you assume that it is 2 MPH or slightly higher. When you buy your artificial lures and they come in a small box, there is important information written on the side of the box. That information will tell you the depths that the lure will dive to under different conditions. The information will be a range of depths like 5 to 15 feet. Lures of this type will go deeper as the trolling speed is increased so a 5 to 15 lure will dive and stay at 5 feet at a very slow troll, like 0.8 MPH and dive to 15 feet at a fast speed like 1.5MPH. The cast distance also affects the dive depth, but the speed is the most important factor. Most anglers do not keep their lures in the original box. When I purchase a new lure, I take it out of its box and immediately take a permanent marking pen and write the dive depth on the lure, usually on the side or belly. If you are like me, as soon as you take the lure from the box, you will throw the box away, so get in the habit of making this note when you open the box. If you forget, there is still an inaccurate way to tell the dive depth. If the lure has a short lip, say ½ inch, it will probably not dive below 5 feet. If the lip extends to an inch or more, the lure will probably dive to more than ten feet. If the lure has no lip, it is probably a surface lure, or jerk bait and is made for casting not for trolling.

One question that is asked repeatedly is the correct depth to fish around a school of bait. It is not unusual to see a school of bait on your sonar while you are searching for game fish or simply trolling. Most game fish, especially bass are always roaming around looking for these bait schools. When they find such a school they will always look for weak, wounded or younger bait fish first. These are the bait fish that are normally trailing along behind the school or dropping away from the school due to their weakness. Bass particularly look for these weak fish and they will strike at them first. If a bass attacks a bait school it will normally attack the top of the school or the trailing edges, it will rarely attach the center of the school. The sonar photo below illustrates a school of shad. This illustration clearly shows the game fish attaching the outer edge and the top of the school.

The game fish attack the school in this manner because if they attacked the center, they would create panic among the bait fish and the school would scatter. The bass want to go in and grab a bait fish and then retreat a short distance to swallow it. They will then attack again for another bait fish. It is easier to get these fish if the school is somewhat intact where the majority of the bait fish don't even know they are being attacked until it is too late.

When you are fishing around a school of bait fish, keep your bait close to the top of the school or sometimes close to the bottom. You want to make the bass think that your bait is one of the struggling bait fish. If you are trolling or casting a distance from the center of the school, which is most common, you should let your bait or lure go deeper so it will appear like a trailing or wounded fish. If you find fish feeding on the bait school as shown above, these fish are gorging on the bait. They will repeatedly attack the school until the school finally realizes what is happening and it will break up.

The procedure I just described sounds simple but is not. Remember, the bait school is likely moving when you first spot it, especially if there are attacking game fish as shown in the illustration. You actually never know what direction the school is moving. A good technique is to start circling the school when you first spot it, changing the diameter of your circle on each rotation. If you spot the school again as you circle, you will get a good idea on their direction of movement and you can follow that direction and better adjust your casts or the position of your trolled bait.

When I am circling a school of bait fish I normally vary my boat speed regularly during the turns to change the depth of the bait and make it stand out from the others in the school. If I am casting around a school, I will finesse my lure in both direction and speed to achieve the same result. The secret is to make your lure or bait stand out from the rest of the fish in the area.

Once you get the knack of depth control, you will soon realize that this method of **Fishing Different** produces more excitement since it will certainly increase your catch rate.

What is The Typical Strike Zone?

I love to answer questions for which there are no obvious answers, because those answers can never be proven right or wrong with facts. It's like telling you that the temperature on a specific day, 200 years from now will average 82 degrees. No one alive today will be around to ever prove me wrong. When asked what the actual strike zone is for fish, I have be honest and say that I don't really know. In fact no matter how experienced an angler might be, there is no real correct answer to the question about the distance of the strike zone for fish. The strike zone is the distance a fish will move to strike your bait or lure. For most large fish there is a general consensus that in clear water, a 30 foot sight distance is attainable at times. Having said that, we then have the modifying factors like water clarity, temperature, time of day, size of the fish, health of the fish and many others. In addition there is the question of sight clarity. A fish might see an image at a distance, but it might not be clear enough to warrant any interest to attack. Of course there is the question of the fish specie. The general configuration of the eye of a fish is similar in most game fish with the eye consisting of biological elements called rods and cones. There is a great deal of difference, however, in the effectiveness of the sight of different species depending on the rod and cone structure of the eye of that particular specie. As an example, some species like walleyes have more cones than rods in their eyes. This makes them more apt to see better at night. If a species has more rods than cones, it will see better in the daylight hours. Then, of course, there is body structure. Some fish are fatter around the head than others, making it more likely their rearward vision might be better than a fish with a slim body and head.

We know that the eye of a fish is similar in many aspects to the human eye, except that fish have no eye lid to open and close as a function of the amount of light entering. Fish eyes are also on the side and upper portion of its head and protrude out of the head providing the fish nearly 180 degree vision in each eye. There is only a small area directly to the rear of a fish that blocks its vision due to the shape of the body. Clearly the best sight range of any fish is directly forward.

We can begin to see why there might not be any specific correct answer to the question of the strike zone. There are two elements of interest to the angler related to this subject. First is the "zone of recognition" where there might be the recognition of an image in the area. That image might not be clear enough to entice the fish to attack but it simply notifies the fish that there is something there.

Coming closer in is the "zone of interest." This is the area where the image is clear enough to draw the interest of the fish. This is also the zone where the other senses of a fish come into play, like the lateral line to sense vibrations or the ability to smell the object. This zone can also not be precisely defined because there are factors that influence it. One such factor, often overlooked by anglers is the number of other fish in the area that are also competing for the same food sources. This is defined as the competition in the area. We do know that when the waters are crowded with other fish, a predator will strike out after food about 50% faster than when there is no competition.

Can we generalize about the strike zone or zone of interest? Yes we can, but that generalization won't do an angler much good. I believe it would be safe to say that if a fine meal is passed within inches of a fish, from an area in front of the fish, it will always strike out after the meal. On the other hand if the same meal is passed 100 feet in front of the fish, it probably will not attack the food. That leaves a great deal of area that remains in question. Let's see if we can be more precise.

We do know that fish do not like to be surprised. If your bait is brought to the fish from its rear quadrant or behind it, the fish will most likely be surprised and dart away from the bait or not show any interest at all. Fish are usually spooked by movements coming at them from behind.

We also know that water temperature plays a big role in defining the distance that a fish will dart out after food. Colder waters of the fall and winter months slow down the metabolism of the fish and cause it to move more slowly. In cold water a fish exerts much more energy attacking its food than it exerts in warm water, thus the fish will be hesitant to attack a longer distance in winter months. The same exact effect is seen in the hot summer months when the water temperature is much higher than the comfort zone of the fish. Under these two extreme, fish are very conscious of the amount of energy that they waste attacking food. This means that in very cold and very hot water bait should be moved very slowly.

These factors become more important if we are fishing in water that contains a current of any measureable speed. Fish at rest will always face upstream because the dynamics of their bodies is such that they attain the best buoyancy with water running over their bodies from front to rear. When fishing where there is current, bait should always be thrown upstream so that when retrieved downstream, it will pass in front of the fish. Also when trolling in non-flowing waters, if you see fish on your sonar and they do not bite, change the direction of your troll and you will also likely change your luck.

Lure color is another misleading factor that many anglers think is the secret to their good luck. The fancy colors and artistic designs placed on today's lures are put there to attract the angler into buying the lure, not to attract the fish. The color and design that we see when the lure is in its box, is not the color and design that the fish sees when the lure enters within its strike zone. Colored items in water change their color and shape. Water distorts shapes and changes colors. Different colors have different wave lengths in the color spectrum and in the water. Some colors disappear in the water sooner than others. Red, as an example, loses its identity at a distance of about 15 feet in the water. Blue, on the other hand, retains its color out to more than 20 feet.

A common ground rule used by anglers for years is to "match the hatch" meaning that lures should have color and shape that is the same as the natural live food in the water. For the most part that means lures should be colored with a predominant grey, silver of white color.

How about flash? It is my opinion that fish are attracted by flash but, of course, they do not eat it. It is really no different than our human reaction. On an overcast day if lightening suddenly appears in the distance, our eyes immediately shift to the direction of the lightening. Emergency vehicles use flashing lights, to attract the attention of people in the area. Flash makes us look in the direction of the flash. The same is true for fish.

Years ago before stores were loaded with hundreds of different lures, we used a lure called a Davis Spinner. I mentioned this lure early in this book because years ago we made our own spinners. The Davis Spinner was actually a complex rig consisting of two or three shiny spoons that spun around as we moved through the water. At the end of the series of spinners there was a leader and whatever bait we chose to use. As the assembly moved through the water the three spinners would create a great deal of flash to attract the attention of the fish. If they looked in the direction of the flash, they would also see the bait trailing behind. The bait was their target, the flash simply attracted their attention.

There are hundreds of lures today that operate with the same principle. The spinner on the front end attracts the attention of the fish but the fish is tempted to strike at the attached bait, not the spinner. There are some lures such as spoons that incorporate both features in a single lure. The spoon creates flash but it is also designed to have some resemblance to a fish. These lures will usually catch fish without any bait added.

The distance of interest with lures that contain flash is slightly longer than lures without the flash, but normally the fish will have to see the bait before it initiates the attack.

Some anglers believe that flash is only effective on sunny days but that is not true. The sun does amplify the flash, but any shiny item in the water will create some amount of flash as long as there is some light present.

In order to not leave the impression that the average strike zone and zone of interest is an unsolvable problem, let me suggest some average numbers that can be used as a guide. On an average day, with a slight ripple on the water surface, in water that is not terribly stained or muddy, you can assume that the strike zone is around 10 feet. In very clear water it might increase to 15 feet and in murky water it might decrease to 6 feet. If you use these distances as a guide, you probably will have a positive outcome. Keep in mind however, that strike zones are totally irrelevant if there are no fish in the general vicinity of where you are fishing. Also, fish are usually a moving target. When you see them on your fish finder and you try to adjust your cast or troll to land within their field of view, they will have used those few seconds to move a good distance from their original position.

With all of the information presented in this chapter, it might seem that I am drifting from the concept of simplicity. Actually in keeping with Einstein's statement, I want you to know all of these seemingly complicated factors, but only so you truly understand that **Fishing Different** is knowing which elements are important and which others are simply supporting facts. The important information to understand is to use the guides I have presented to put your bait or lure above the fish and carefully control its speed and direction. If you do that, everything else will fall into place naturally.

CHAPTER NINE

The Glamour of the Moon

"The saddest aspect of life right now is that science gathers knowledge faster that society gathers wisdom."

Isaac Asimov

The moon has always been there, hanging in the sky like a never ending light. Referring back to an earlier chapter, it was certainly there when Gronk and his Neanderthal community looked to the skies for the guidance of their Gods. They probably were confused by the changing nature of this light that sometimes glowed bright in all its glory and then slowly disappeared into the darkness of the night. It would be hard to imagine that the Neanderthals were intelligent enough to relate the brightness of the moon to the rising and falling of the ocean's waters that sometimes permitted them to retrieve more fish for food.

The moon has a special meaning to me. My career as an engineer and later a corporate executive was spent with an aerospace company that was awarded the responsibility for designing and building the Lunar Module, that carried three Astronauts to the moon and back. Nearly ten years of my career were involved in this program. Those years were climaxed on July 29, 1969 when astronauts Neil Armstrong, Buzz Aldren and Mike Collins landed our vehicle safely on this mysterious heavenly body. For thousands of engineers and executives, this achievement was to be the highlight of their careers, for it was likely they would never again work on a project that offered such a challenge of the unknown.

Even today, after the United States has sent several landing parties to the Moon and dozens of unmanned probes, the Moon still offers us a great deal of mystery in terms of exactly what it does to affect our lives here on Earth. The Moon is the single subject that has split the fishing community right down the middle with one side carrying a strong belief that the position of the Moon relative to the Earth has a significant effect on the behavior of fish and the other side feeling that this is simply a myth that has grown out of proportion over the years. I subscribe to the later theory.

There are many things that science can prove or disprove about the moon. When it is not possible to obtain scientific proof usually it involves a subject where nature enters the picture since nature itself often causes behavior among animals and plants that is confusing to pure scientists. There are many examples of this phenomenon.

European badgers are known to pee more during periods of a new moon. Corals off the coast of Australia produce a massive release of eggs and sperm during a period near a full moon. Cats and dogs are said to get into more mischief during a full moon. Lions which rarely hunt during the daylight hours will start killing during the day when the moon is full. Scorpions start to glow in the dark during a period of a new moon. All of these are based on reports, not organized scientific studies or testing. We must therefore assume that these occurrences were observed, but we have no idea how many times they happened or the validity and conditions of the observations. Unfortunately, observations such as these have often been raised to a level of credibility and adopted as accepted rather than proven theories.

The same doubts surround the idea that the positions of the Moon relative to the Earth cause behavioral changes in freshwater fish. It is scientific fact that the gravitational pull of the Moon on Earth causes tidal changes in the oceans. This phenomenon has been studied to such an extent that the rise and fall of the ocean tides can be absolutely correlated to the position of the Moon relative to the earth. These movements can be calculated and are published as tidal tables.

Tidal changes in the oceans cause disruptions in the ground surface beneath the water causing the release of organisms and aquatic life sources that become food for the many species of salt water fish. I would not question that the position of the moon has a significant effect on the behavior of salt water fish and perhaps on some freshwater fish that live in rivers that are affected by the tides. These behavioral changes of the fish, however, cannot be carried over to freshwater fish. Even though the idea of the Moon effecting freshwater fish behavior has been widely accepted among anglers, I have been able to find no scientific proof that shows how and why that occurs. The applicability of the work that was done is questionable at best. Let me summarize that work.

In 1926 an investigator named John Alden Knight came up with a theory that he applied to all wildlife. Since Knight was an avid fisherman, he slanted his studies toward fish behavior. Knight's studies indicated that there were 33 factors that he believed affected the general behavior of fish and wildlife, especially their feeding habits. For fish he quickly eliminated all but three of these factors. He then concluded that the remaining three factors were the Sun, the tides and the Moon. Of course for freshwater fish we can rule out the tides, except as previously noted. In 1936 Knight published the first Solunar Tables which many anglers accepted as a proven theory, but the theory was never proven by tests or comprehensive data collection. Solunar tables have since that time been included in nearly every fishing publication and taken as gospel by half the anglers in the United States and many other countries.

There have been other experiments since Knight first published his tables. A biologist at Northwestern University, Dr. Frank Brown, conducted a test using oysters. Brown had data that indicated that oysters open their shells during each high tide. Again here we are talking about a salt water species. Brown wanted to know if the shell openings were an effect of the tidal change or the Moon position. He had fresh live oysters shipped to his laboratory in Chicago which was a long distance from any salt water. He sealed the oysters off from any sunlight while they were in the water. For the first two weeks of the experiment, the oysters continued to open their shells during the same time period that the tide was high in their home ocean. During the third week of the experiment, the oysters opened their shells during a time period when the Moon was either directly above or under their current position in Chicago. These are the two studies that have formed the basis for the myths of the Moon's effect on fish behavior.

When I published my first book titled "Jake's Take on The Lake" in 2007, I first challenged the validity of the Solunar Tables because I could find no credible information that proved their authenticity. Since that time there have been others who have joined in the discussion.

A fishing guide named Joe Bucher had been keeping a detailed record of all of his fish catches for his daily guided fishing trips. Bucher had thousands of catches that formed the basis for his conclusions. He compared this catch information with the fishing times listed in the Solunar Tables and he came to the conclusion that there was no validity to the "best times" listed in these tables. His correlation with the tables was less than 10% overall. Bucher further studied his data and found a fairly good correlation between the active fish bite and the time that the sun rose and fell. That conclusion coincides with the popular belief that the best time of the day to fish is shortly after sunrise and shortly before sunset. Most experienced anglers accept that premise. I have discussed this theory briefly in Chapter Four.

Another more recent finding published in an article titled "Casting Beyond The Moon" written by Professor Mike Allen, sought to determine with empirical data, the validity of the Solunar Tables. Allen and his friend Porter Hall had data for more than 450 bass catches. Most of this data was for bigger bass in the 10 pound range. Allen took this data and attempted to correlate it with the times published in the tables for the dates when the fish were caught. Allen's total correlation was less than 21%. Full Moon correlation was 28%, while the two other Moon phases accounted for 21% and 27%. This type of correlation would never be considered a valid affirmation that the Solunar Tables are accurate.

With published evidence mounting, I decided to join the group of non-believers and run a series of tests myself. On three different fishing trips, I selected 12 days where I fished the entire day. I wanted to be sure that I didn't bias the results with incomplete days of fishing. Since I do less nighttime fishing I selected five nights where I fished several hours during the night. The number of night samples is less because some of the places that I fished did not permit fishing after sunset. When the data was completely recorded I went back into the Solunar Tables and compared my results with those listed in the published tables.

The twelve daytime trips produced 729 fish, mostly bass. The night trips produced 40 fish of the same species. The data from the daytime fishing is shown below.

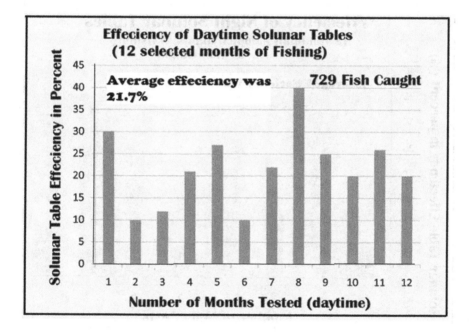

When the catches were compared against the recommended best fishing times the correlation was only 21.7% meaning that only 21.7% of the fish that I caught were caught during the recommended good fishing times of the Solunar Tables. I feel that a fish catch of 729 fish is a good statistical sample to claim legitimate results.

The nighttime fishing results were slightly less conclusive due to the smaller sample of fishing nights and also a smaller sample of fish caught. The nighttime results are shown below.

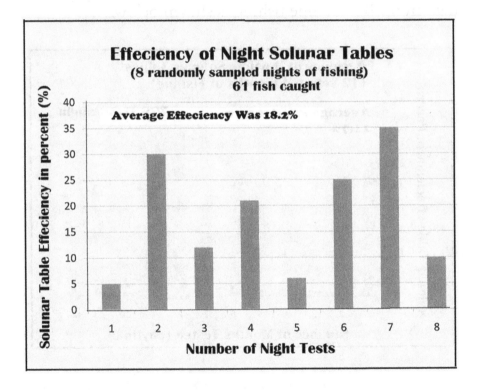

The correlation of these nighttime catches with the Solunar Tables was 18.2% which is even less convincing than the daytime results.

Readers should be reminded that if I were to have picked a fishing time randomly out of a hat and indicated that time to be the best for fishing, then I flipped a coin to determine if that was the right or wrong time, with enough flips, the resulting probability would be 50% that I had picked the right time. Any controlled tests that show correlations in the 20% to 30% range would never be considered statistically valid.

Since no one I have been able to find has given any valid proof that the Moon's position is a good predictor of the best fishing times, we must accept the negative results discussed here as a fairly convincing argument that it is a waste of time to use these Solunar tables to guide your fishing times.

What are the Best Times to Catch Fish?

Now that I have attempted to burst the bubble of the Solunar Tables, what is an angler to do to determine the best times of the day or the best times of the month to catch fish? Another long standing theory about fishing times indicates that shortly after sunrise and shortly before sunset are the best times of the day to fish. Baitfish schools tend to move to the shallow water as the sun sets in the evening and then they move out to deeper water as the sun rises in the morning. Wherever the bait schools go, so go the predators so I have no argument that early morning and early evening are good times to fish. The problem I have with this theory is that the belief is so strong in some fishing circles that many anglers don't bother to fish during the middle of the day.

In chapter one I stated that it is my opinion that the penetration of the Sun through the water is the single most important factor effecting fish behavior. If this theory is correct, it supports the thought that early morning and early evening fishing times are best. It does not mean that fishing cannot also be good at other times during the day. I know many anglers who will not bother fishing during the middle of the day because they have been convinced that the fish don't bite during those times. These anglers are simply wasting a lot of good fishing time because fish can be caught at all hours of the day and the mid-day hours are often the best times to fish depending on the weather condition.

I have been part of a family fishing team that visits Canada twice each year to catch different species of fish. As an outdoor author I have also had the opportunity to travel to many locations in the United States. When I travel to fish these new areas, I record every catch that I make, so that I can study the results to prove or disprove theories and myths that have developed through the years. The following data represent some of the results of these studies. I only used data from those days where I fished from sun up until sun down. The trip shown below resulted in a catch of 80 smallmouth bass and 8 muskies caught in four days of fishing.

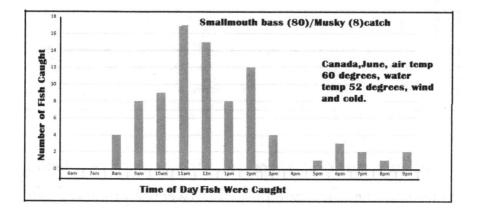

These results show that the majority of the fish were caught between 8 am and 4 pm, with neither time representing sun-up nor sun-down. The absence of any catches during the 4 pm hour was the result of a quick stop to eat dinner.

The second series of data that I examined was a trip on a North Carolina lake where I fished a complete day from 7 am until 8 pm for three days. This lake produced only largemouth and spotted bass. Both of these species are known to be active eaters in the early morning hours. Let's see what the data tells us.

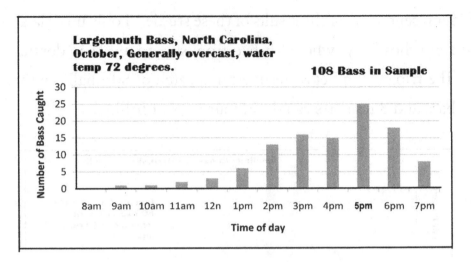

Largemouth Bass, North Carolina, October, Generally overcast, water temp 72 degrees.

108 Bass in Sample

What a surprise! There was little or no action before 11am and the catch rate peeked between 2 pm and 6 pm. Notice the absence of sunrise catches.

To further investigate my new discoveries I examined the data from another northern trip where northern pike was the specie sought. The results of this 174 northern pike catch are shown below.

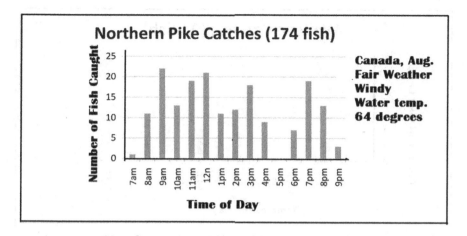

Again the catch rate was fairly consistent through the mid day hours. The absence of any 5pm catch was again due to taking a dinner break. The sunrise and sunset theory is partially confirmed in this data except that the mid-day catch was still heavy.

The last specie that I tested was walleye. This species is known to be very sensitive to sunlight and it was at least partially sunny each day of this trip. With the exception of a shore lunch and dinner break, the walleye catch was consistent throughout the day as shown below.

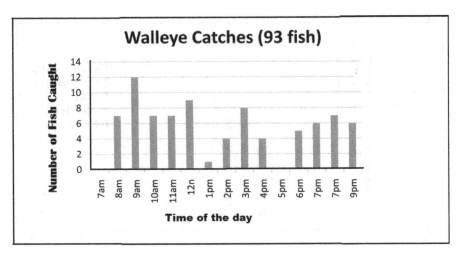

There were several hundred fish catches in my data including 93 walleyes, enough to draw some meaningful conclusions. I don't want to argue the sunrise and sunset theory although this data does not strongly support it. The major point of this research is that any specie of fish can be caught at any hour of the day and the data definitely shows that fishing during the middle hours of the day can be very productive. The key to understanding this data is to understand that as the sun rises in the sky on relatively clear days, your fishing technique has to change. If the sun is penetrating the water, fishing must be deeper in the water column and around structure and boulders. Using jigs and other deep water lures helps during high sun penetration. If the weather is windy and the water surface is broken by waves, there is less cause to change your technique since the broken water surface provides a great deal of disruption of the sun's rays.

I recently completed a study of the times that I caught fish during full day fishing over a period of the last five years. The results are illustrated below.

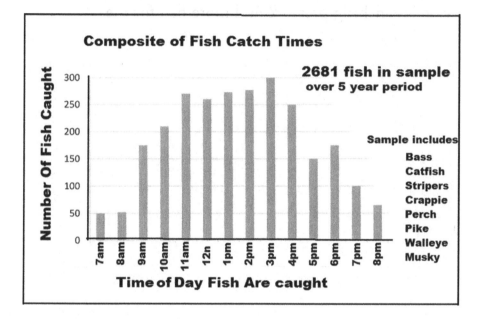

Friends and associates have often criticized me for being an afternoon angler. I justify my case for **Fishing Different** with this sample of 2681 fish caught. No need to get up early with the majority of my fish being caught during the middle of the day.

No one can effectively argue that a sample size of 2681 fish is not a valid statistical sample. This data should convince even the most doubtful angler that **Fishing Different** during the middle of the day produces good results. For those who continue to doubt these results, please stay off the water during the mid-day hours. It will mean less fishing pressure and more fish for me.

CHAPTER TEN

The Role of Sound in Your Fishing Experience

"There are no limits to growth because there are no limits to human intelligence, imagination and wonder."

Ronald Regan

One element of our fishing processes I believe has advanced significantly due to man's quest to understand rather than simply accept is the element of sound. Noise was always a no-no when it related to the angler. During those early learning days I described in the Introduction, I was always taught that everything done inside the fishing experience had to be cloaked in silence. Sound, as I was instructed, would spook the fish and send them scurrying away from my fishing location. I was just never interested in challenging this concept.

About six years ago I was fishing for stripers on Lake Norman with David Clubb, a friend and striper guide.

David was born and raised on that lake and he knew the habits of every species of fish residing there. The striper bite was very slow that morning. David was frustrated because he was seeing many stripers on his sonar equipment but he couldn't get them to take our bait.

After several minutes of tolerating this situation, David picked up what looked like a sawed off baseball bat. He began slowly pounding this club on the bottom of his metal John boat. As he continued the gentle pounding, he kept a sharp eye on the sonar screen and sure enough the stripers began to come closer to the surface, apparently to investigate the sound. It wasn't long before those stripers began to hit our lines. "Works all the time" David laughed, "these fish were lethargic just hanging around deep in the water column, they were bored and when they heard the repeated pounding they just had to come up to determine where the noise was coming from."

I had heard of this practice before but I thought it was simply one of those myths that had developed over the years with no real scientific proof behind it. "It really doesn't work every time" David muttered, "but it's exciting when it does."

Over the course of the next several months, I tried that practice myself but I could never get the same results. It wasn't because I wasn't pounding properly, but because every time I saw striper images on my sonar, they always seemed to be in a feeding mood and I can't complain about that. The whole experience however got me thinking about noise as it relates to fresh water fishing. Over the course of writing my previous six books about fishing, I continued to research the subject of noise because I was beginning to see evidence that the lure industry was starting to incorporate noise making capability in some of their lures. At this point I simply had to acquire a better understanding of the science behind the noise theory and I went fairly deep into my research on the subject.

In some of my previous books I skirted the edges of the noise subject. My work with sonar image interpretation led me to develop my theory about "dentrails" that are left behind as a fish swims through the water. These dentrails become visible on a sonar screen and I wanted to know why. That led me to study material about cavitation which I believe is the cause of these dentrails. Cavitation is caused by the rapid movement of the tail of a fish which leaves air voids or bubbles that are detectible on most sonar screens. Three years ago I was asked to design a statistically valid testing program to validate the workings of a new piece of equipment called a Hydrowave, which simulates the sounds of schools of bait fish. This equipment was designed to excite otherwise lethargic bass. Most recently my friend Mac Byrum, a catfishing expert came up with the design of a new rig that would catch catfish and nearly any other species of fish. This new rig which Byrum named the "catch-all rig" uses a surface lure with spinning blades on its front and rear, and is trolled as a deep water lure but held off the bottom by its tendency to seek the surface. This new rig is discussed further later in this book.

As I began to deal with all of these elements individually, I realized that they all had a common connection and that was the lateral line of every fish. Without the lateral line, none of these concepts or products would work.

I will describe each of the above concepts and hardware here, but for a better understanding of each, I have to start with the lateral line. We have all heard of the lateral line but to totally understand how and why it works is complicated. I will attempt to simplify the discussion as much as possible.

The Amazing Lateral Line

I stated earlier in this book that some of the actions and reactions of fish and other animals can only be explained as gifts from Nature. Nature has provided fish with many capabilities that could not previously be explained scientifically. In recent years as we have become more inquisitive about the unknowns in life, we have gotten deeper into the puzzles of Nature. We have known for many years that the brain of a fish is very small when compared to the brains of other living things. That knowledge led us to also believe that this small brain was unable to process many of the relatively simple signals that other brains could handle. These facts are true but on the other side of this story, there are things that the brain of a fish can do that continue to amaze scientists. The functioning of the lateral line is one of those mysteries.

Fish and some amphibious animals have been provided with a very unique sensory capability called the lateral line system. Using today's modern jargon, we might even say that this system provides the fish "virtual" detection capability. It permits them to virtually touch something without actually making contact with the object. This capability recently became a popular subject by a group of

German scientists who believe that a better understanding of this system could, through biometric engineering, better equip robots to orient themselves in varying environments. The studies of this group of scientists have provided us with some amazing facts about the functioning of the lateral line system.

One conclusion the group has developed is that we humans take in and process only a small portion of the information that surrounds us at all times. Infrared light, electromagnetic waves and ultrasound are a few examples of external influences that humans can grasp only with the help of external technological measuring devices. Some animals can use special sense organs, their own biological equipment, for that purpose. This is what the German group is attempting to better understand.

Here are some examples. In very murky water which is barely penetrated by light, pike and pickerel can feel out their prey before making contact with them. The blind Mexican cave fish can virtually feel structures and can avoid obstacles where there is no light. Catfish can follow invisible tracks that eventually lead them to their prey. The lateral line system registers changes in current and even smaller disturbances, providing backup support for the sense of sight in dark and muddy waters.

The lateral line system runs along the left and right side of most fish from the gill cover to the tail. It is sometimes also located around the eyes and mouth of the fish. To simplify a very complicated discussion, the lateral line consists of a canal of water running under the skin of the fish from front to rear. Detectors called neuromasts connect to this canal and are themselves connected to hair cells which transmit signals to the brain when there is the slightest change in the external surrounding of the fish. These hair cells are similar to the cells in the inner ear of humans that process sound and other signals to the brain. The hair cells transmit signals to the brain that permits the brain to determine the causes of unusual disturbances, such as another fish swimming by or another fish in close proximity.

These latest studies validate some of my early findings that led me to define the "dentrail" left behind by every swimming fish. The studies proved that a swimming fish produces vibrations or waves and leaves eddies behind its swim path. The German scientists defined these eddies as a "vortex street" and it lasts for about a minute after the fish passes. This "vortex street," which I have previously labeled as the "dentrail," of a moving fish can be detected by a quality sonar fish finding system. I will discuss "dentrails" later in this chapter.

The lateral line studies currently being done have already led to several significant conclusions. One such conclusion indicates that a fish can reliably fix the position of another fish in terms of a distance corresponding to their own body length. Each fish broadcasts definite and distinguishing information about itself into the field of currents. If a predator fish detects the presence of a possible prey, it can determine if that prey is of a size that makes it worth pursuing as a meal.

Perhaps the most astonishing finding of the German scientists is that the lateral line of a predator fish can actually measure the angular coordinate from its swimming path to the path of a prey and the brain of that predator can adjust its swimming path to directly attack the prey. This capability is considered to be far beyond the processing capability of the human brain.

There have been other studies that have theorized that small schooling fish, if sensing they are being pursued by a predator, will begin to swim in perfect unison which can alter their signature and make it look like they are a single large fish rather than a school of smaller fish. This would tend to scare off the predator. I have not seen the results of that study and I have doubts that small bait fish would have already developed that intelligence.

The Concept of "Dentrails"

In my book "Beneath the Surface" which was published in 2009, I introduced the concept of "dentrails" that often show up on a standard sonar fish finder display screen. Most anglers look to their sonar screens to show bottom structure, bait fish schools or game fish images. Those are all important images, but there is a great deal of additional information on that screen that is also very important for a better understanding what is going on beneath the surface of the water. One such information source is the dentrail left behind a swimming fish. I describe this phenomenon as seeing something that is not there. The term dentrail comes from my aviation days and those beautiful white trails of condensation trailing behind a jet aircraft flying at high altitude. The hot exhaust from the engines hits the cold high altitude air causing condensation trails called contrails. There is a similar phenomenon taking place behind a swimming fish except that the trail is not condensation but density. As a fish accelerates through the water, it uses its caudal fin (tail) to exert pressure against the surrounding water. The vector forces exerted on the water on either side of the fish tend to cancel out laterally but generate a net force forward that propels the fish through the water.

In its simplest form, I theorized that this continual motion of the tail of the fish, especially when the fish is accelerating or swimming somewhat erratically, produces small air bubbles or voids behind the fish. These voids create a small pocket of air that has a different density than the surrounding water. The density difference is reflected in the return sonar signal and appears on the sonar screen as a broken or dotted line. Since the line is caused by differences in density, I defined it as a "dentrail".

A dentrail in its simplest form might appear as shown in the following photo of a sonar screen

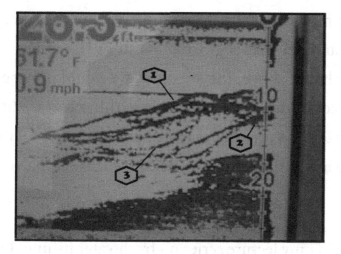

In this sonar image, two actual fish images are marked as number 1 and show up as high density targets as evidenced by the heavy solid marking. Dentrails are shown as numbers 2 and 3. The heavier dentrail marked number 2 indicates that the fish was swimming out of the picture, leaving behind a strong trail of voids or bubbles. The dentrail marked number 3 is another fish that is not shown on the image that is no longer in the view of the sonar scan. Other dotted lines also indicate the presence of other swimming fish. Although only two solid fish images are visible here, there are at least five other fish that have left the area. There are times when the images of several dentrails appear on the sonar screen and no actual fish images are visible. These are still useful images since they indicate that fish are in the area but have left the field of view of the sonar scan. Many anglers forget that the image displayed on the screen only covers an area that is 1/3 the depth of the water. For the image shown above, the area in view would only be about seven feet in diameter. Dentrails within view are fish that are outside this area but may still be fairly close to the boat, so they are within a region making them reachable by the angler.

During my lecture series on freshwater fishing, I receive many doubting comments about dentrails from anglers who attend these lectures. As time passes, some anglers actually comment that they are now buying into the concept because they have seen the value. Others still remain skeptical. I became encouraged in 2013 when the winter issue of **In Fisherman** was released. In that issue, Doug Stange, the magazine's Editor-In-Chief, wrote an article titled **The Language of the Predator**. The article focused on the sensing capability of the lateral line of a fish. Stange's position is that every fish creates hydrodynamic vortices as they swim through the water. He theorizes that these vortices are different for each species of fish depending on their size and water conditions. He calls these vortices "fish footprints". Stange believes that predator fish can actually detect these footprints through their lateral line and can determine the specie of the fish by the specific footprint of that specie. This detection capability permits the predator fish to follow the footprint trail of its prey.

Stange's position is a strong support to my theory of the creation of "dentrails." At first I had doubts about the concept of individual fish footprints, but after reading the material published by the German scientists that we discussed above, I now support that theory.

One challenger of my theory recently asked me to define exactly, the content of the air bubbles or voids. He believed that without an understanding of the chemical content of the bubbles, it was illogical to conclude that they could be detected by a sonar pulse return. My answer was relatively simple. Sonar sound waves are very susceptible to differences in density of the object causing the beam reflection. The density of water is approximately 1.0 g/cm^3. Air or a void in the water has a density of about .0012g/cm^3. This tremendous difference in density would surely be detectable by a pulse of sound from a sonar transmitter sending sound waves through the water. Even though the reflected signal would not indicate a solid object such as a fish, it would be processed as an object because of the significant difference in density. If the fish was moving forward fast enough to create voids, these voids would appear as dots moving through the water in the same pattern as the fish that was generating the image. If only one air bubble was present, it would not be discernible on the sonar screen. When a fish is swimming continuously, a trail of bubbles follows the fish and can be easily recognized on the screen.

Undaunted by my critics, I continued to search for other evidence that my theory of "dentrails" was valid. I discovered a paper written for the Journal of The Royal Society, by G. Iosilevskii and D. Weihs, titled **Speed Limits On Swimming Of Fishes And Cetaceans.** I was searching for material discussing "cavitation" since my years of experience as an aerospace engineer and pilot reminded me that voids of the type I was discussing were caused by cavitations. Cavitations in the aeronautics world are critically important because airfoil designers are always worried about leading and trailing edges of airfoils, since the speed of air above and below an airplane's wing is what determines its ability to fly.

In water cavitations are the formation of vapor cavities that are the result of forces acting on the water. They are small liquid free zones, bubbles or voids in the liquid. Cavitation usually happens when a liquid is subjected to a rapid change in pressure. There are two types of cavitation, inertial cavitation and non-inertial cavitation. Inertial cavitation is the process where a void or bubble in a liquid rapidly collapses, producing a minute shock wave. Non-inertial cavitation is the process in which a bubble in a fluid is forced to collapse in size due to the application of outside energy.

Cavitations caused by a fish swimming through the water are inertial cavitations that result from the rapidly changing presure on the water caused as the tail moves rapidly from side to side. The faster the tail moves, the greater the pressure change and the bigger the cavitation. As the fish moves away from the initial point of pressure change, the pressure differential gets lower and lower until the voids or bubbles eventually disappear.

It is possible that this phenomnon also includes an element of non-inertial cavitation since the voids are being hit by the sound waves from the sonar unit. The sound waves are an external force being applied to the voids, possibly causing them to change size, shape, or even burst from the external force of the sound waves. In either the inertial or non-inertial form, the cavitations from the fish are easily visible on sonar screens when fish are swimming rapidly through the water.

The study referred to above was not looking to define my dentrail theory, but it did contain some great work to determine the leading and trailing edge characteristics of the caudal fin of fish, that might limit the maximum speed that a fish can obtain in the water. The article contained the definitions of relationships between lift, drag and the area and shape of the caudal fin of a fish. These relationships were mathematically defined as they related to cavitations that might be caused as the fish swims through the water. As I read this paper, the first thing that came to my attention was the illustration which I have extracted to show below.

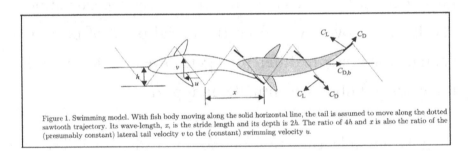

Figure 1. Swimming model. With fish body moving along the solid horizontal line, the tail is assumed to move along the dotted sawtooth trajectory. Its wave-length, x, is the stride length and its depth is $2h$. The ratio of $4h$ and x is also the ratio of the (presumably constant) lateral tail velocity v to the (constant) swimming velocity u.

This simple illustration and the text that followed drew me to the conclusion that I might find evidence here that cavitations and the creation of voids or bubbles was indeed a valid theory. I do not expect my readers to grasp the technical details of this work because I have not yet absorbed it all myself. But in aerospace terminology the words that I have extracted below are critical to my dentrail theory.

"Stall in an airfoil...is caused by boundary layer separation from the foil surface. The boundary layer separates either due to an unfavorable pressure gradient over the leeward surface of the fin, or due to appearance of vapor bubbles, forming whenever the surface pressure drops below the vapor pressure of the liquid in which the fin moves. This later phenomenon is known as cavitation."

The authors go on to define mathematically, many of the relationships, causes and effects of cavitations on the ability of fish to reach certain speeds. It serves no purpose here to include those mathematics.

It was certainly not the purpose of the research done and presented by Iosilevskii and Weihs to prove my theory about existence of dentrails. They made no mention of the detection of the cavitation voids or bubbles by sonar sound pulses. The research does, however, validate my theory that the swimming motion of the tail or caudal fin of a fish can and under some circumstances does, cause cavitation voids or bubbles. Their research even goes as far as to state that these voids move downstream to the direction of the fish and that the voids will eventually collapse. Under some conditions, if this collapse occurs at or very close to the fin, damage to the fin may actually take place. This is part of the authors conclusion that the speed that a fish can achieve is often limited by its aerodynamic and hydrodynamic characteristics and the conditions of the water in which the fish swims.

The only portion of my theory of the creation of dentrails that I have not proven conclusively is the element that deals with the ability of a sonar sensor to detect the density differences between water and cavitation voids.

When questioned on this matter, I often refer to a common sonar image that is seen in areas where cold spring water enters a water body which is at a much higher ambient temperature. I have included a photo of this image in Chapter Seven.

The most interesting aspect of dentrails to me is the possible sound that dentrails make in the water. We have all heard the sound of air bubbles in a boiling pot, or the sound of bubbles when air is blown into a glass of water through a straw. The sound we hear is actually the bubbles breaking into the air. What is the sound of those air bubbles that break under water?

Think about a school of shad swimming through the water. There could be as many as 5000 shad in a school, swimming in a circular pattern and moving through the water. Each of these small shad is leaving a dentrail behind it. The individual dentrails are masked by the volume of the fish, so those dentrails simply blend into the overall sonar image, but they are still there, in the water, to be heard by all of the predator fish that are interested in chasing them.

One theory has been advanced by the recent developers of the Hydrowave. This is a small electronic instrument that transmits noises into the water that are supposed to be the noises made by schools of shad, herring and shiners. The developers of the Hydrowave actually recorded noises from bait schools and then duplicated these noises electronically. The theory behind the Hydrowave is that lethargic bass that might not otherwise be interested in biting will be stimulated by hearing the sound of schools of bait fish and actually move in the direction of the sound. So let's see if there is any validity to this new sound theory.

Examining The Hydrowave

A recent addition to the line of available technical angling products is the Hydrowave. The concept of the

Hydrowave is that this equipment generates the sounds made by schooling fish of different species. There are a variety of different sounds for each specie like the sound that they make when at rest, in a frenzy etc. By transmitting these sounds into the water it is presumed that otherwise inactive predator fish will be alerted by the sounds and become active in their search for the bait school.

The scientific theory behind the development of this equipment is consistent with the sound making capability of bait schools discussed above. The following scientific background was taken in part from the sales documentation for this product.

Tactile Sound Transmission (TST) is the primary output of the Hydrowave's speaker system. Finely tuned amplifiers deliver the tactile sound. Tactile sound is different from ordinary sound because it is sound that you can actually feel. The concept is easy. If you are wearing earplugs or other sound blocking elements, you will not be able to hear people talking around you, but you can feel the sound of a sub-woofer speaker system. Fish hear on that same type of tactile level and frequency. The same frequency and sound is produced by the Hydrowave. The Hydrowave incorporates sounds in two different ways, Lateral Reactive Technology (LRT) and Vibration Reactive Technology (VRT).

Lateral Reactive Technology (LRT) is a vibration wave technology that operates at a frequency level that stimulates the predatory response through a lateral line of the fish. As with any predator, fish are stimulated to the presence of prey. A fish can receive this stimulation through its lateral line. The lateral line is naturally tuned to detect a frequency range of 1 to 80 cycles which is the range generated by small prey fish such as herring, minnows and others. The Hydrowave generates these vibrations to create a predatory response.

Vibratory reactive technology (VRT) is a vibration wave that operates at a frequency that stimulates a predatory response from fish through their inner ear. Contrary to popular belief, fish do have ears. The ear of a fish is not like the ear of a human. Instead of funneling the sound like a human, a fish ear consists of dense bones under the skin that detects and translates vibrations. This vibration detection is so accurate that a bass is completely able to differentiate between vibrations from prey and other sources.

The vibration patterns used in the Hydrowave are the natural patterns from natural sources of prey. Minnows, shad, herring and schooling bass fry are the primary vibration patterns. Other vibration patterns resemble water displacement associated with feeding and schooling fish.

Because my books and my research blend the science of fishing with the sport of fishing, the inventors of the Hydrowave asked me to do some independent testing to verify the effectiveness of the equipment. A summary of my findings follows.

The Hydrowave was tested under a variety of conditions in both cold and warm water months. The test results illustrated the benefits of the Hydrowave for increasing the catch rate for Largemouth Bass and Spotted Bass. The cold water catch rate was 1.62 times higher when the unit was on compared to the rate with the unit off. In warm water conditions the catch rate was 2.23 times higher when the Hydrowave was on compared to when it was off. Based on these test results, the author must conclude that the Hydrowave definitely works in terms of increasing the catch rate for bass.

A complimentary Hydrowave unit was provided to the writer in December of 2011 with the intent to provide a series of controlled tests to determine the effectiveness of the unit under a series of different fishing conditions. Since the receipt of the equipment was in the colder winter months in North Carolina, the initial series of test were conducted during December, January and February on Lake Norman in western North Carolina. The authors fishing procedure during these colder months is to troll, using a 16 foot pontoon boat. The first series of tests used this fishing method and boat. The author understood that this fishing procedure was not the procedure for which the Hydrowave was designed. The author felt that it would be a good test of the basic theory of the Hydrowave, if it was used under conditions different from its intended mission.

The initial plan was to switch to a different fishing mode in the spring months when the water warmed and the bass moved to the shallower water. At that time the Hydrowave was switched to an 18.5 foot Sea Chaser boat, where the fishing technique was to be the traditional casting around docks and other structure.

There was initially a third phase of testing planned, where the unit was to be used in Canada while fishing for smallmouth bass, but that phase was cancelled due to scheduling conflicts.

The procedure used was to record all catch activity during times when the author was fishing during the testing period. The unit was turned on for a period of one hour then turned off for the same time period. This was repeated on each day of fishing. Most fishing days consisted of at least four hours, so there were two opportunities on each day for the unit to be on and the same time period for the unit to be off. The fishing procedure, bait, weather and all other factors were always the same on a given day of fishing so that the catch rate would not be influenced by external factors such as weather, water temperature or fishing procedure. Records were kept of all fish caught including catfish, crappie and perch, but only the largemouth and spotted bass were counted in the test results. During the entire test period, 95% of the fish caught were bass so there was no opportunity to determine if the Hydrowave had any effect on the other fish species.

During all of the test periods, both boats used fish-finding sonar equipment, both Lowrance 332c sonar units. Hundreds of sonar image photos were taken using a digital camera to get data on fish activity when catches were made. Sonar image photos were also taken of any bait schools that were spotted in the immediate fishing area that might also influence the results. Recording bait school activity would also indicate if the sounds emitted by the Hydrowave were having any effect on the bait schools in the area.

During the initial cold water tests, there were 30 days of testing, not all sequential. Five of the initial tests were discounted due to the suspicion that the unit had become disconnected, leaving 25 individual days of cold water testing. During this first phase, there were 100 hours of fishing with nearly equal on and off time for the Hydrowave. When the unit was on, the individual settings of sound were varied randomly, so there are no results based on the most or least effective bait school sounds. During these first phase cold water tests, there were 156 bass caught, 100 bass caught with the unit on and 56 caught with the unit off. The test results for the first phase of testing are shown below.

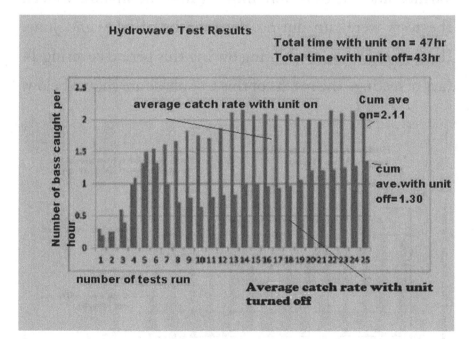

These results indicate that the cumulative catch rate when the Hydrowave was on was 2.11 per hour. The cumulative catch rate when the unit was off was 1.30 per hour. This would make the catch rate 1.62 times better when the Hydrowave was turned on.

Water temperature and barometric pressure were carefully monitored during these tests and evaluation showed that the variations in these two elements appeared to have no effect on the catch rate

During the second phase of the testing, the waters had warmed and the bass were moving into the shallow waters. The tests were run during the months of May and June. There were 58 hours of testing during this period covering 14 days of testing. The results of this test phase are shown below.

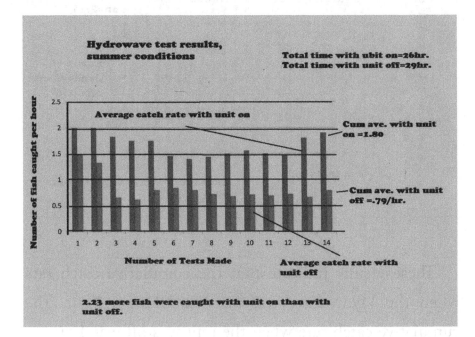

The results shown above indicate that during the times that the Hydrowave was turned on (29 hours) there were 47 bass caught for a cumulative catch rate of 1.80 per hour. During the 29 hours that the Hydrowave was turned off, there were 23 bass caught for a cumulative catch rate of 0.79 per hour. This indicates a catch rate 2.23 times larger when the Hydrowave was on compared to when it was off.

Because the shad had schooled during the warmer months, there were many more shad schools visible during the second phase of the test periods. There were some repeated indications that the shad schools had a tendency to scatter when the Hydrowave was turned on. This was observed several times but it is possible that the bass in the area were the cause of the shad schools scattering. In either case shad school scatter was a definite observation.

Most of the fish caught were measured and photographed to determine if there was any difference in the size of the fish caught with the Hydrowave on, compared to when it was off. There appeared to be no difference in size. Catch rates for both unit conditions were slightly better at times when there were large schools of shad in the area during the warm weather months. This was an expected situation. There were a few instances when the sonar indicated that fish had risen in the water column to investigate the sound source, and then descended again when no bait was observed.

It is obvious from my testing of the Hydrowave, that sound generating techniques and equipment are very effective in stimulating predator fish to react to the artificially generated sounds. Anglers must understand that underwater events are very complicated and it is a combination of several factors and events that define the complete angling experience. As an example, the lateral line of a fish plays the important role in the long range detection of forage fish schools. Other aspect such as the strike zone, define when other senses such as sight and smell kick in. Sight is usually the final sense that completes the predators attack. We may have wondered how blind or wounded fish survive in the competitive underwater environment. Vibration detection may explain that phenomenon, but it is rare that a predator fish will make an aggressive attack without seeing its prey.

This chapter has presented a great deal of detailed and perhaps interesting science about how noise effects fish behavior. Unfortunately it is difficult to derive definite conclusions of how a typical angler can use this information to gain better angler success. As Ronald Regan states, perhaps all of this great intelligence leads to more imagination and wonder but I feel it is more than that. Vibrations are detected by fish. Lures that emit sound and vibrating pulses are more detectable by fish than those that are silent. Since studying this subject I have started using more split lures and swim baits that have vibrating characteristic when dragged through the water. I use more lures with spinners and propellers to create vibrations. I do not carry a baseball bat on my boats and I still suggest that my fishing guests keep their voices to a mild level. There is a great deal more that we have to learn about sound but from all of the information that has been gathered to date, this is an area that needs a great deal more study. The potential of new findings could have a very significant effect on fishing processes in the future and may cause many of us to start fishing different.

CHAPTER ELEVEN

Choosing Your Preferred Angling Technique

"Anyone who has never made a mistake has never tried anything new"

Albert Einstein

When Gronk the Neanderthal first discovered that fish could be caught using clams as bait, he and his clan were confined to fishing from the shores of Lake Turcana so their fishing style was similarly simple. There were no other choices available to them at the time. It was probably at least one generation beyond Gronk that discovered moving the bait would catch more fish. We will never know how many more generations would progress before the Neanderthals discovered the possibility of fishing from a raft or a crude boat.

I am a firm believer that every sport has a history and an evolution. When I learned of the discovery of the first fish hook back more than 42,000 years ago, I became curious to know how long it took for that knowledge to develop into the sport of fishing. Obviously, information about happenings that far back in history can only be pieced together by historians from bits and pieces that are discovered and begin to form a story.

We learned that the Neanderthals eventually found they could catch fish a distance from the shoreline by using vines to get their bait out further into the water. How long might it have taken before those same primitive humanoids realized that if they could themselves find a way out into the deeper water, they might catch larger fish? The obvious answer to that question lies in knowledge of when the first floating boats might have been constructed.

A cursory examination of documented history indicates that the first known boat was probably built about 8000 years ago in Nigeria and has become known as the Dufuna Canoe. It got that name because particles from the boat were found in the Dufuna village on the Komadugu River. The discovery of the boat's remains was made in 1987 by a Fulani herdsman while digging a well. The material was tested by several different Radio-Carbon techniques and verified that the African mahogany wood dated back more than 8000 years. This made the boat the oldest in Africa and probably the oldest in the world. In archaeological terms this date is described as an early phase of the Later Stone Age which began about 12,000 years ago.

Prior to the discovery of the Dufuna Canoe, it was previously believed that the oldest known boat was the Pess canoe, a dugout made from the trunk of a tree. It was estimated that this canoe was constructed about the same time as the Dufuna Canoe. It is assumed that because of the small size of these canoes, they were probably used for fishing rather than for transportation.

The first ocean going boat is estimated to have been built about 7000 years ago and portions of this boat were found in a very unlikely place: the Kuwaiti desert. The ocean going boats which have been discovered were assumed to be built primarily for transportation up and down the large rivers since they were much larger than the earlier canoes.

The point of this brief excursion through history is to show that it probably took at least hundreds of years for early mankind to discover that both sport and necessity could be served by vessels that could bring the angler closer to where the bigger fish lived.

Having read the introduction to this book, you are aware that my introduction to fishing at a very young age did not involve a boat, so the question of my angling style in those early days is very simply. I simply sat on the bank of a large pond with my bait suspended by a bobber and waited for a fish to come along. That's all I knew at that time so, to me, there was no other choice of angling style.

Later in the introduction, I described the next phase of my fishing education when we built our first boat. To me, that was graduating to the big leagues. With a boat we could catch the big ones by trolling for hours, searching for trout. Looking back on those experiences I realized that fishing from a boat didn't produce more fish, but it produced bigger fish. This was one of my early learning experiences.

As I further developed my interest in fishing, I realized that it probably was not the boat that gave us bigger fish it was the lake fishing versus pond fishing. There were simply larger fish in the lake than there were in that stocked trout pond.

Many anglers today consider casting or trolling as their only available angling styles: an angler is either one who casts or one who trolls. TV and other media usually show professional anglers casting for the big bass. That has set the common image of an angler who trolls as somewhat of an offbeat character. Of course, this is not true. Anglers who simply enjoy the thrill of fishing have several alternatives available to them. Some of these techniques are variations of casting or trolling and others have an identity all their own.

Still fishing is perhaps the oldest and most versatile angling style. You can still fish from the shore like I did as a beginner, you can fish from a dock or pier or you can still fish from an anchored boat which is perhaps the most popular technique. Still fishing can be done both with the bait on or off the bottom and will catch just about every species of fish. The secret of still fishing of course is to find the fish. If you are still fishing in an area where no fish are located, this becomes the most boring of all the angling techniques.

Drift Fishing permits you to use your still fishing techniques but in this case the boat is not anchored and drifts through the water pushed by either the current or the wind. Drift fishing permits a great deal of flexibility. You can fish off the bottom or use a bobber to select a position within the water column. Jigging can be very effective while drift fishing and you can use just about any type of bait although natural baits like worms or live bait fish work best. While drift fishing, you have the flexibility to cast a lure if you see fish activity in the vicinity of the boat.

Live Lining is a technique normally used when fishing in flowing water like a stream or river. With this technique the boat is anchored and the bait is moved down-stream from the boat by the flowing current. The use of live bait is best for live lining.

Bottom Bouncing is a variation of drift fishing and is used where bottom structure is significant like rocks and boulders. This is a technique for locating fish from a drifting or trolling boat. Your bait is dragged along the bottom as the boat drifts. The dragging motion causes the lure to bounce along the bottom often stirring up the bottom silt or sand. This sometimes gives the effect of crawfish running along the bottom stirring up small clouds of silt. Once the first bite is achieved, it is wise to anchor the boat to more thoroughly fish that area.

Jigging is a very popular technique for fishing some species of fish such as walleyes and crappie. When jigging you simply cast the jig out and let it settle to the bottom or near the bottom. Movement of the rod tip up and down presents the jig or bait as the image of a struggling fish that would be easy prey for the predator fish. Jigging is best performed from a boat that is not moving so that the jig can move vertically up and down. Slight movement of the boat will permit effective jigging but the jig becomes more effective when it is moved vertically. If the jig is tipped with a worm or other live bait, it can be cast a distance from the boat and allowed to sink close to the bottom. Before the jig reaches the bottom it can be retrieved slowly creating a sweeping movement of the bait across the bottom.

The techniques just described are all accepted methods of catching fish under different conditions in different types of water. Most anglers have used one or more of these techniques but several surveys that have been taken still show the vast majority of freshwater anglers define their angling technique as one of casting or trolling or a combination of both.

A simple way to begin to grasp the concepts of trolling and casting is to understand the role of both styles. Trolling is considered the best way to find the fish and casting is considered the best way to catch the fish. This implies that an experienced angled uses both techniques on a regular basis, using whichever technique is right for the occasion. The occasion can be the type of water being fished, the specific specie being sought, the weather and water conditions, the structure of the water body and much more. With the exception of the professional anglers who earn their living competing in tournaments, most other anglers use a combination of both trolling and casting. Since fishing tournaments are usually time-restricted, professional anglers normally use their practice days to search for the bigger fish and then want to optimize their angling time during the tournament by casting in areas where they believe the bigger fish are located. These professionals have many electronic aids to help them locate the fish during the practice sessions. Since the majority of published tournaments involve bass fishing, professionals have studied the behavior of bass thoroughly and have concluded that casting produces the most and biggest fish for them.

That is not exactly true for all species of fish and for every water body. As an example, it is rare to observe a fisherman casting for a catfish. It is known that catfish will occasionally strike a lure, but the normal habitat for catfish suggests that deeper water slow trolling is the best technique to use for success with all species of catfish.

Crappie are a specie that normally desire variations of both styles. Trolling small live bait through an area with structure will be successful with crappie. A more popular technique involves small jigs that are sometimes cast but more often simply jigged or fished with a bobber to achieve slight motion. Some anglers have achieved great success trolling or drifting with several rods tipped with these jigs.

A common technique for fishing for pike and muskies in northern waters is trolling to search for the growth areas that might hide these monsters and then casting toward the growth to lure the fish out. One of the most exciting times in any angling experience is to cast a spoon toward the edge of a bed of weeds and see a monster pike or musky burst up out of the water to grab the lure. These fish have also been known to follow your retrieve right up to the boat, only to grab it an instant before you pull the lure up for another cast.

Walleye are a specie that are also known to react to both a trolled lure or bait or a controlled jig. Since walleye are normally found in groups, finding them with a trolled lure or live leech and then sitting on top of the group and jigging usually produces good results.

Stripers and hybrids are normally caught by trolling live bait or a moving lure. If stripers are moving in large schools, they are usually looking for schools of bait fish. When they find and strike a school of fish and create visible surface action, casting into that activity will always catch fish.

Many anglers are not seeking one specific species of fish and the few species I have described above will react to either technique under different conditions so let's look at when and how each technique may work best.

Casting is usually best suited for the shallower water and when you have pinpointed your target fish either by eye or by a sonar detector. If you find a large rock or other large structure in fairly shallow water, you can be fairly confident that there is a fish close by. If you troll close by that structure you will likely spook the fish. If you stand off 30 or 40 feet and make several casts toward the object, you will probably have success. In shallow or very confined areas, casting is your best bet.

There are times when you observe fish on your sonar that seem to be suspended in deeper water and will not bite a moving or trolled lure. It's always worth finding a deep diving lure and casting it toward the area where the fish were seen. Sometimes just the noise of the splash of the lure hitting the water will activate a lethargic fish.

Trolling seems to work best in the summer and fall seasons when the fish are spread out. Trolling in shallow water will work in these instances but it must be a very quiet and slow troll.

A good criterion for determining whether to cast or troll is, if you are in shallow water cast and if fish are spread out troll. Better yet use a combination of both by searching for the fish by trolling and cast once they have been found. Remember, each of these techniques is simply a different method of presenting your bait to the fish. If they react to one or the other technique, stick with that technique until there are no longer biting fish, then either change to the other method or search for another area to fish.

Normally when fishing in a large water body, if the fish are located below the 20 foot level of depth, you will probably not reach them with a casted lure. That same lure trolled a little faster might get you down an extra 4 or 5 feet. If that deeper level seems to be predominant for that water body, you would be better advised to use a rig such as a Carolina rig where you can control the depth by adding or subtracting weight to the rig.

One situation where trolling is almost demanded, is in a high wind condition. It's very difficult to cast to a targeted spot in high winds. In very high winds, even a good quality trolling motor is sometimes hard to control. Safety should always be a consideration but windy conditions usually dictate trolling.

This is a good spot to add a safety hint. Most trolling motors are not designed to be run at maximum speed for long periods of time. If you have to use your trolling motor at high speeds, make sure you make periodic slow-downs to let the motor cool. I personally had one situation where my main motor failed and I decided to use my trolling motor to get me back to the dock, 300 yards away, I ran the trolling motor at high speeds constantly and it got so hot that the main control cable actually melted.

I have been asked on many occasions if trolling or casting requires a specific kind of equipment. My answer is usually no, then I qualify my answer. The type of equipment you use is more a function of the type of fish being sought. The larger fish are usually fished with casting combinations because they are thought of as being more rugged. The truth is that either spinning or casting equipment will usually work in every situation. There are however considerations that will lead you to the right equipment selection. If you are in a situation where you wish to make very long casts and precision is not important, spinning equipment is normally best. If you are fishing in close quarters and you need more precision with your casts, bait casting equipment works best.

Your equipment selection might also vary with your experience level. Most inexperienced anglers prefer spinning equipment because it is slightly easier to use. In fact some standing myths about casting equipment have directed inexperienced anglers away from casting equipment. Indeed you must develop some skill to properly use casting equipment but with knowledge of your equipment and a small amount of practice, once you get the knack of a casting set-up, you will likely never go back to spinning gear.

Since the real enjoyment of any type of fishing is the retrieval process, you will want to select equipment that gives you the best feel for the fish when it is being retrieved. You should try to select equipment that provides you the lightest and most flexible feel for the specie being sought so that you can experience every movement of the fighting fish. To me, this is the real joy of **Fishing Different.**

Boat and Bait Speed

Whether trolling or casting, I have observed that there is a great deal of confusion about the proper speed to move bait through the water. Many anglers feel that bait speed is related to the swimming speed of the fish specie they are after. Fish swimming speed may have a minor influence on the speed at which you move your bait, but it is only a minor effect. Most freshwater fish have swim speeds between 8 and 12 MPH and some can accelerate to 20 mph for short periods. This would indicate that bait speed is not influenced by the ability of the fish to catch-up with the bait but is influenced by other factors. Among these factors are water temperature, water clarity, bait flash, bait color and most importantly, the mood of the fish at the moment the bait approaches.

With all these possible effects, it would seem that it is impossible to set a good average bait speed since the variables will constantly change or are unpredictable. As an example, when casting a lure the bait movement will be affected by the structure around which the fish are hiding. It is not unusual for a fish to pass up a lure on the first observation since this observation only grabs its attention. The attack will normally take place on the second or subsequent cast. Small fish which are the preferred prey of most predator fish usually skirmish around structure at different speeds. They will make a fast dart and then slow or stop. Since common practice is to match the hatch, lures that are cast around structure should also be made to move in a similar fashion. Speed in most casting situations is a function of the reel gear ratio, the turning habit of the angler, and the amount of finesse that the angler chooses to apply to the rod and lure.

One aspect of bait movement that is often misunderstood, particularly among part time anglers, is the gear ratio of their reels. Professional anglers pay attention to this factor since they are casting and retrieving lures day after day, and it important to them to know exactly how fast their normal crank rate is moving the lure. A high gear ratio of 7.1 or 8.1 to one will take up about 30 inches of line with every turn of the handle. This ratio then produces a lure speed of about 1.6 MPH. A medium gear ratio of 6.1 to 6.4 to one will take up about 25 inches with each turn of the handle creating a lure speed of about 1.4 MPH. A low gear ratio of 5.1 to 5.4 to one will retrieve about 20 inches of line for a retrieve rate of about 1.2 MPH. These retrieval speeds, of course, can be increased by a much faster turning rate on the reel. On average I have always advised anglers to assume that one turn of their reel retrieves about two feet of line for an average retrieve rate of about 1.5 MPH. This assumes that the turn rate of the reel handle is about one turn per second. If you double that turn rate to two turns per second the bait speed will be about 2.7 MPH.

Unfortunately the issue of gear ratio can get much too complicated for the average angler. Most of us have probably purchased reels without concern for the actual ratio so it is probably more useful to identify gear ratios with their recommended lure usage. I have categorized the three classes of gear ratios and the consensus opinions of the lures that are best used with those reels as follows.

Low Gear Ratios (5.1/1-5.4/1)
> Deep diving crank baits
> Large swim baits
> Deep water spinnerbaits

Medium Gear Ratios (6.1/1-6.4/1)
> Squarebilled Crank baits)
> Medium depth crank baits
> Shallow depth spinnerbaits

High Gear Ratio (7.1/1-8.1/1)

> Jigs and big worms
>
> Shaky heads
>
> Texas rigs
>
> Carolina rigs
>
> Top water lures
>
> Jerk bait lures
>
> Lipless Crank Baits

Each of the above ratios and lure types can also be affected by the angler's retrieval style which can be steady, variable speed or start and stop.

Water temperature is a very important factor for determining bait speed. In very cold water below 50 degrees F, the metabolism change in the body of a fish makes the fish very hesitant to rapidly strike out for food. Nature has taught the fish that the amount of protein gained from one bait fish is not worth the amount of energy expended. This dictates that slow bait movement is required in colder weather. The converse of course is also true when the water warms, a faster bait movement might be effective.

Lure speeds for most artificial lures are an element of the lure design. Most lures are designed with a particular movement speed in mind. Many crank baits, as an example, are designed with different length and shape front end bills (noses). These bills combine with lure speed to determine the depth at which the lure will swim. On lures of this type, the faster the lure moves, the deeper it will swim.

Segmented swim baits with several breaks in the body are also designed to perform best at a specific speed that will make the lure move like a live fish. Spinner baits are designed to produce flash to attract the attention of the fish. The faster the lure is moved the greater the flash of the spinners. Spoons and other lures have design speeds that are also optimized for the specific application. Some of the manufacturer-suggested lure speeds for different lure configurations are shown below.

Spoons	1.8-3.0 MPH
Flashers	1.5-3.0 MPH
Crank Baits	1.5-6.0 MPH
Wobblers	1.5-3.0 MPH
Spinners	0.5-1.5 MPH

These recommended speeds should be adjusted faster for warm water and slower for cold water. Lures with flies attached should be retrieved at between 0.3 and 0.5 MPH.

In general the average speed for trolling lures is between 2.0 and 6.0 MPH.

There is some published data suggesting speeds for retrieval of bait for different species of fish. These retrieval speeds are shown below.

Walleye	1.25-2.5 MPH
Bass	0.5-2.0 MPH
Muskies	2.0-4.0 MPH
Stripers	0.5-2.5 MPH
Crappie	0.5-1.5 MPH
Trout	1.0-3.0 MPH

I must offer caution here to remind readers that there are so many variables that effect this information that each angling situation warrants a trial and error process. I have found that constant variation of bait speeds is the best way to determine how you can activate a fish in the area you are fishing.

There is a contradiction associated with this data. Scientists have suggested that cold water dictates a slower bait movement. The data above however suggests that fish such as walleye, muskies, and pike that are normally considered as cold water fish seem to like bait movement that is higher than the suggested speeds for the freshwater species. This illustrates that even the experts who prepared this information are uncertain of its accuracy.

There is another consideration that effects troll or retrieve speed for bait. Using live bait requires that the bait be moved no faster than about 0.8 MPH. When live bait is pulled faster than that it tends to spin and take on an abnormal swim movement. The best trolling speed for live bait is between 0.4 and 0.8 MPH. This speed difference between live bait and lures illustrates why it is not advisable to troll live bait and lures at the same time. Trolling at the ideal lure speeds will render the live bait somewhat useless. Conversely trolling at the optimum speed for live bait will be too slow for proper action of the lure.

Now that I have confused you with all of what might be called the "politically correct" information, let me try to simplify all of this for you. As for reel gear ratios, use whatever you have. If you are shopping for new gear, use this information as a guide to match the situation that you will most often face.

Retrieval speed for lures and trolling speed for lures or live bait is fairly important. If you are casting, assume that you are cranking at one turn per second and that retrieval speed will be fine. Apply variations of speed and finesse. If you are trolling, use speeds of between ½ and 1 MPH as an average for live bait and around 2 MPH for lures. Move bait faster in warm weather and slower in cold weather. Use deep diving lures during high sunlight periods and shallow or top water in early morning hours. If fish are in the area and not biting, vary your speeds and try smaller lures or baits.

Most inexperienced anglers most likely have chosen their particular angling technique or settled on their choice of equipment. The information presented above is not intended to confuse anyone, but more to illustrate that there are many considerations offering opportunities for **fishing different.**

CHAPTER TWELVE

Variety is the Spice of Life

"If a man does his best what else is there?"

General George Patton

Most part time anglers tend to develop a liking for one or another fishing style. Their equipment represents their selected style and they usually use the same accessories like hooks, rigs and lures every time they fish. There is nothing wrong with this pattern, especially if it continues to produce acceptable results. I have found however, that sticking to the same routine over and over again tends to lead to boring fishing experiences, especially if you fish on a regular basis or you are thinking about **Fishing Different.**

Trying something different doesn't necessarily mean changing equipment, bait or your overall fishing style. There are times when a simple change in bait or lure presentation will turn a bad day around. I'll give you one example.

We were fishing on a lake in Ontario, Canada in early spring. The lake was loaded with smallmouth bass but on this particular day they just didn't want to bite. It's not unusual on this lake for an angler to catch and release 40 or 50 bass in one day, which would be an average catch. Not getting a bite in the first couple hours of fishing was certainly not acceptable.

We had decided to start fishing over some big boulders that were submerged in about twenty feet of water. We could see fish around the rocks on our fish finding equipment but we were not able to bring them up to hit our lures. We tried many different lures, both top and deep water types but still no luck. On one cast over the boulders, my fishing partner Ron Jurcy had a slight backlash and it took him a few seconds to clear it. As soon as the line tightened and he began to retrieve the lure, which was sitting on the surface, the lure was crushed by a large bass.

Ron didn't say anything but he had a hunch that the slight delay in his retrieval was the secret so on his next cast he let the lure set on the surface for a second or two before he retrieved it. Sure enough, another bass hit the lure. Apparently the lure hitting the water attracted the attention of the fish and when the lure started to move, it was time for the fish to react.

We both switched to that slight hesitation in our retrieve and we had great success for the remainder of the day, as long as we were fishing around submerged boulders. We changes lures several times and that seemed to make no difference. As long as we used the hesitation, the fish hit the lure.

We have all heard the expression "there is more than one way to skin a cat." I'm certainly not suggesting that any, one go out and try skinning a cat, but I do believe that fishing enjoyment can be increased if the angler tries several of the techniques available. In the previous chapter I discussed some of the differences between trolling and casting. Switching from spinning gear to casting gear is a big leap for most beginner anglers. A somewhat less traumatic experience is learning to use different set-ups or rigs. A well rounded angler should understand many of the other standard rigs that are used for different fishing situations. I will discuss some of the most widely used rigs in this section

Methods of Rigging

Every time I think I have learned all of the methods of creating a design for terminal tackle, called the rigging, someone comes up with a new type of configuration. Rigging terminal tackle elements simply means putting the various pieces together in a configuration best suited for the type of fishing and the type of fish that are being sought. I'm going to cover the most common rigs used today, for bank and dock fishing as well as fishing from a boat. Let's start with the simplest rigs. There are three basic rigs shown in the illustration below.

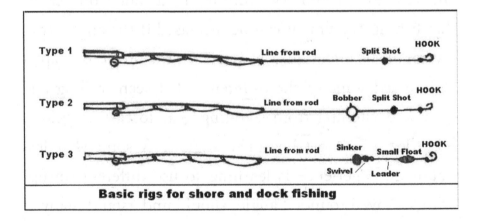

Basic rigs for shore and dock fishing

The first rig labeled type 1 is the very simplest and uses a hook and a small split shot as a weight to get the bait on or near the bottom. In this case the split shot will bring the bait down, and any movement of the bait will be permitted by the small section of line or leader between the split shot and the hook, normally about 12 inches long. If you are using live bait, this short leader will permit the bait to move around attracting the attention of the predator fish. This simple rig would be used mostly in shallow water.

The second rig labeled type 2 would be effective when using a bobber in deeper water where you desire to keep the bait up off of the bottom. The depth of the bait is set by the distance between the hook and the bobber. For ease of casting this rig and retrieving a fish, it is suggested that the distance from the bobber to the hook not be more than the length of the rod.

The third rig labeled type 3 is used when you want your bait near the bottom but not resting on the bottom, and you want the bait to have freedom to move around. In this case a slightly larger sinker would be used to rest firmly on the bottom. A swivel is used to attach a leader from the swivel to the hook. This small section is often called the shock leader. The shock leader is normally about 2 to 3 feet long. A small float or bobber is attached here about 10 inches from the hook. The size of the float should be only large enough to keep the bait floating, but not so large that it will pull the sinker up off of the bottom. This rig is normally used with live bait because the bait has the freedom to move around freely. In this case again, the total distance from the sinker to the bait should be only slightly longer than the rod.

Another simple rigging method often used while fishing from a boat, which can also be used when fishing from a dock in deeper water, is the **drop shot** rig shown below.

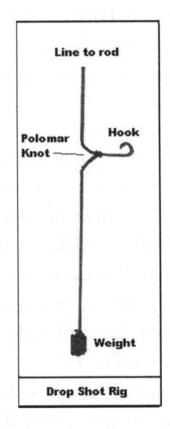

The **drop shot** rig is a technique first used by anglers to catch suspended fish. This rig gave them the opportunity to put their bait at exactly the depth that the fish were at. In recent years this rig has also become popular for other fish that are suspended such as walleye, crappie and some pan fish. The **drop shot** rig is a way to tie your hook up the line where desired with the weight solidly on the bottom. The technique used is to cast or drop the rig over the side and let out line until slack is obtained. Reel up the line until it is tight, then start lightly jiggling the rod tip or moving it side to side. The weights used are normally between ½ and ¾ ounce and always less than 1 ounce. Bait can be any form of plastic bait or live bait. The Palomar knot is recommended since it provides double strength. The hook should be sized to the species of fish being sought.

A rig common to bottom fishing whether from a boat or dock is the **three way** rig shown below.

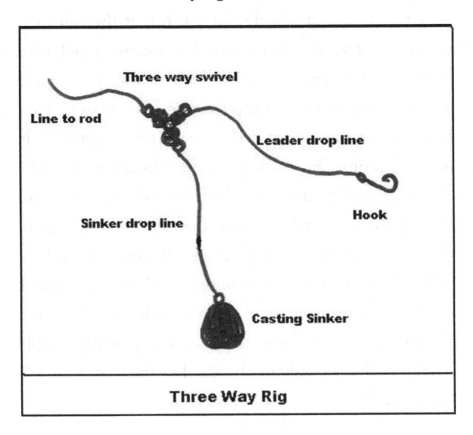

Three Way Rig

This rig receives its name from the three way swivel which is the center of the rig. All aspects of this rig are rigid and any changes in depth or line distance have to be made prior to use. These rigs are used mainly for areas with flowing water such as streams or rivers. The indicator of a bite with this rig is the rod tip which will move when a fish moves the bait. For this reason you are advised to keep the main line fairly tight once the sinker has reached the bottom. In swift water, keep as little slack as possible on the main line so that you can see or feel the bite. This rig has several variations and can be used with different type weights for different situations. The rig can be trolled by replacing the casting sinker with several split shots or a slinky weight. I will show other variations of this rig later when describing catfish rigs.

Perhaps the most simple of the popular bass rigs is the **Texas Rig.** The **Texas Rig** is shown in the photo below.

Texas Rig

This rig is considered a finesse rig meaning it is the action of the angler rather than the action of the lure that makes this rig work. The rig is flexible in that it can accommodate almost any type of plastic bait, and because the plastic hook up makes the rig weedless, it is popular for use around vegetation and brush. The rig is cast and slack line permits the rig to flow down to the bottom. If a fish is in the area it will often hit the bait before it hits the bottom. If this does not happen, let the rig sink to the bottom, then start to retrieve it slowly with short jerks of the rod tip. This makes the plastic bait jump up as it is retrieved. Once the retrieve has begun, the line should be kept tight with very little slack. It sometimes takes a little practice to distinguish a bite from a bump on the bottom. Because the plastic is covering the hook, when a bite is felt, the hook must be set with a forceful snap of the rod to pull the hook through the plastic and into the fish. A bead can be used between the hook and the bullet weight if desired and many anglers keep the bullet weight in place by forcing a small toothpick into one end, breaking it off once in. The weight size for fairly shallow water less than 20 feet deep is between ⅛and ¼ ounce. For deeper water a slightly heavier weight may be better.

One of the most popular rigs used today by almost all anglers is the **Carolina Rig,** which is shown in the photo below.

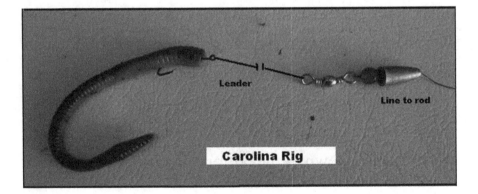

Leader

Line to rod

Carolina Rig

The reason for the popularity of this rig is that it can be used when casting or trolling and has three important characteristics; it provides a stable attachment point for the bait whether live or artificial, it provides separation and flexibility between the bait and the line, and it provides the bait as much freedom as needed to move naturally through the water. This rig can be used for fishing most any species of freshwater fish. It can be cast and slowly dragged along the bottom. It can be cast and slowly retrieved or it can be trolled. The only limitation of the Carolina Rig is that it should not be used in thick brush or underwater structure. The swivel should be as small as possible for the size of the fish expected and the weight is determined by the depth of the water being fished or the depth at which the fish are suspended if trolling. The shock leader is normally made of fluorocarbon and for trolling, it should be of slightly less strength that the line being used. This is to insure if a hook up occurs, the leader will break before the line breaks, causing only the hook to be lost and not the entire rig. The length of the leader is optional but it is normally between 18 and 36 inches.

A great deal of excitement was created in the fishing community with the introduction of the **Alabama Rig**. The rig, shown below, has been designed to simulate a small school of bait fish swimming through the water.

Some anglers were surprised at the controversy associated with this rig since it is smaller, but an exact replica of the umbrella rig that has been in existence for many years. The umbrella rig was designed for deep water trolling using heavy fishing gear and it has been successfully used for many years.

The Alabama Rig in theory can be used as a trolling or casting rig. The image of several small swimming fish is intended to capture the attention of the predator fish, more specifically bass. It has been successful in its purpose and many anglers are using the rig with great success. Some professional fishing organizations have banned the use of this rig in professional competition. These organizations believe that it violates the principals of sporting competition and also has a tendency to wound fish that attack it and get tangled in one or more of the five hooks the rig contains.

The advantage of the Alabama Rig is that it does attract bass and other predator fish and is successful in catching fish either singly or in multiples. There are, however, disadvantages to using this rig. First, it is expensive for the non-professional angler. The rig at retail costs in the range of $15 with no jigs or bait attached. Then you have to attach 5 jigs and five plastic minnows or other artificial baits so when complete you have a rig costing more than $25.

Another disadvantage of this rig is its weight. When completely rigged, it usually weighs over two ounces in most configurations, making it impossible to use with medium or light fishing gear. Casting this rig, fully loaded is a chore, especially over a period of several hours. Trolling the Alabama Rig makes a little more sense, or at least is less tiring to the angler. When trolling this rig it is necessary to know exactly what depth the rig is at, so that you can keep it from getting hooked up and lost. I have developed a series of curves shown below to assist in keeping the rig off the bottom. This chart will also help the angler keep the rig at the desired depth by increasing or decreasing the speed of the boat. This chart was developed for a medium size rig. The numbers will differ for a lighter or heavier rig and you should make a few sample runs with your rig and adjust the numbers accordingly.

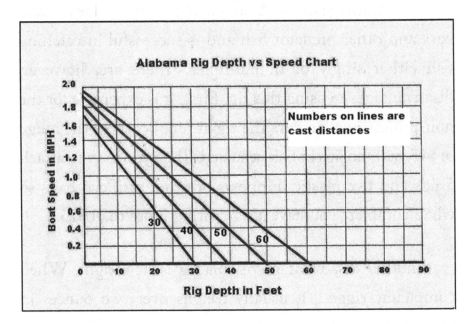

The best way to control the cast distance when using this chart is to feed the rig out manually, measuring the distance the rig is hand fed out to the desired position. Once the desired cast distance is achieved, the depth of the rig is controlled by varying the boat speed, increasing the speed to raise the rig and decreasing it to lower the rig to a deeper depth. Trolling with the Alabama Rig requires that you pay attention to the water depth because the five hooks are in constant search of bottom debris to get hung on.

There will be hang ups both with trolling and casting, so it is necessary to use braided line to get more line strength to release hang ups. This also dictates the use of a Palomar knot and braided line. Making a Palomar knot with a complicated rig such as this is very difficult if not impossible. That makes it necessary to use a clip-swivel device at the end of the line, which is easily tied with a Palomar knot. The clip device is then attached to the end of the rig making the entire combination a little heavier.

There is also evidence from examination of many of the fish that have been caught with this rig, that the fish are aggressively attacking the rig and getting hooked in parts of their body that causes wounds to the fish. This fact is feeding the opponents of the rig, but wounds are also often inflicted by common artificial lures such as crank bait lures that have several treble hooks and also sometimes inflict wounds on the side of the fish.

Another challenge using this rig is that you must try to find jig heads that are very light weight and at the same time have hooks that are large enough and strong enough to handle aggressive bass. I found that I didn't have this type of jig in my equipment box and had to buy a complete set of new and lighter jig heads.

I really do not recommend the Alabama Rig for inexperienced anglers, but I do believe it's worth a try for those who are more experienced and do not mind risking the loss of a $25 lure.

I have discovered a replacement for the Alabama rig called the Booyah Boo Rig, produced by the Booyah Bait Company. This rig contains most of the basic elements of the Alabama Rig but only has one lure attached. The advantage of this lure is that it contains four separate spinners for creating flash and simulating small bait fish and a single trailing line to attach a small lure. The retail cost is about seven dollars.

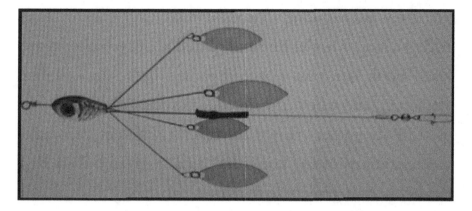

The head of this lure has a weight of approximately one ounce so it can be cast more easily than the Alabama Rig. I have been successful with this lure using a small jerk or crank bait attached to the extended line. I have used it for both casting and trolling and had reasonable success catching spotted bass and largemouth bass.

The Sabiki Rig has gained most of its popularity over the past five years. Anglers who were looking for a simple way to catch live bait discovered this rig as their solution. As more and more anglers began to use this rig, they discovered it was also good for catching any fish that normally ate small insects.

The Sabiki Rig can be fished from boats, docks, piers and any other structure that extends out over the water. The rig consists of several small hooks, each tied to a short drop line a few inched long. The individual drop lines are then tied to a longer leader line and spaced about 6 inches apart. Each hook is normally accompanied by a small fly-like attractant, and when completed looks somewhat like a lure used by fly anglers. There are several different decorative configurations of the hooks but on any given Sabiki Rig, the hook arrangement is the same.

In theory, when submerged into the water, the rig gives the impression of a group of insects, or even very small fry fish swimming in the water. This, of course, attracts the bigger fish. The rig, shown below, is lowered into the water, brought down quickly by a weight tied to the bottom of the rig. When purchased, the rig has no weight attached and must be added by the angler. Some anglers choose to replace the weight with a small lure or spoon to act as another hooking device. The rig is raised and lowered in the water with slow gentle movements. It can also be left at one depth and the hook moved by gentle movements of the rod tip. If there are small fish in the area they will begin to get hooked. When the angler feels the rig load up, the jig is raised and the fish removed. No real skill is required here.

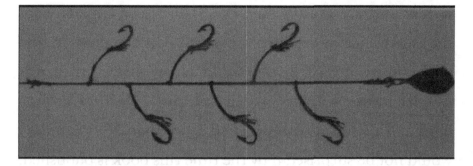

Although the Sabiki Rig was first thought of as a rig for catching small bait fish, in waters heavily populated by other game fish such as perch or bass, the rig has gained popularity for catching those fish also.

There are two cautions when using the Sabiki Rig. First the small hooks are very sharp and can easily stick the finger of the angler. Also with several of these small hooks on one rig, it tangles easily. Any angler who regularly uses Sabiki Rigs is advised to consider purchasing a Sabiki rod. This rod is hollow with a funnel-like tip. When retrieved, the hooks are pulled into the body of the rod and out of danger of hooking the angler or tangling something close by. The Sabiki rod is heavy and stiff and may be uncomfortable for most anglers.

Catfish angling has been growing in popularity all around the country. Catfish are available in most warm waters and are always hungry. Also, many anglers want the experience of catching a big fish. Catfish provide that opportunity. In 2012, the world record blue catfish was caught in Kerr Lake on the Virginia/North Carolina border. This record fish weighed more than 139 pounds. I would not be surprised if by the time this book is published, that record might be broken again.

One of my recent books, "The Catfish Hunters," describes many research fishing trips my co-author Mac Byrum and I made to fully understand the different techniques being used by anglers throughout the United States to catch monster catfish. The techniques and riggings used for this species can be seen in that book.

For this book I want only to briefly describe the most popular rigs that are used for the angling situations that occur most often, fishing from a bank or dock, anchored from a boat, and trolling or drifting in a boat. I have already described the Carolina Rig that is a universal rig used for catching several species of fish. Different versions of the Carolina Rig are also used for catching catfish. The rigs used for catfish are designed to accommodate the eating habits of the three species that are most popular, the blue, channel and flathead catfish. These catfish like to take their food and munch on it before they decide on making it a meal. This is especially true with the blue and flathead species. Once they take a test bite or two, they either spit out the food or swallow it and move on. This dictates that the rigs used to fish for catfish provide the flexibility permitting the fish to take the bait, without feeling the pressures of the line.

The most common rig is the one shown below and is used for still fishing from shore or a dock, or when anchored in a boat.

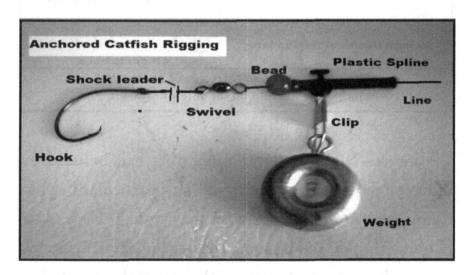

The weight used is the size considered appropriate for the conditions. A heavy weight, such as the one shown, is used in strong currents or heavy wind conditions where the rig needs to be firmly held to the bottom. The plastic spline permits the baited hook to move away from the weight as far as the angler wishes to permit it. This allows the bait to be free for the fish to take its test bites. The shock leader, swivel and bead serve the same function as they do in all other rigs. Typical shock leader lengths are two to three feet.

A typical rig for fishing for catfish from a boat while moving, either drifting or trolling, is shown below.

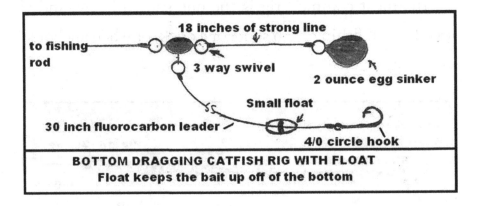

18 inches of strong line

to fishing rod

3 way swivel

2 ounce egg sinker

Small float

30 inch fluorocarbon leader

4/0 circle hook

BOTTOM DRAGGING CATFISH RIG WITH FLOAT
Float keeps the bait up off of the bottom

This rig has several variations that can be used for different situations. When trolling, particularly when fishing for blue catfish, you want the bait to be close to but not dragging on the bottom. The version shown here lets the weight go to the bottom with a small three inch float attached to the shock leader that keeps the bait up off the bottom a distance slightly less than the length of the leader itself. The float should be about ten inches from the hook and bait. Again here, the fish has the freedom to test the bait without immediately feeling the pressure of the line. If you desire to get the bait closer to the bottom, you simply remove the float and permit the buoyancy of the bait to keep it up off of the bottom.

If you know that catfish are in the area but they seem reluctant to bite, which is often the case in very cold water, you can add a couple of spinners and beads between the float and the hook. This provides a small amount of flash as an attractor to the fish.

Catfish can also be caught using a drop shot rig, described earlier and can be caught using a simple Carolina Rig, trolling either live or dead bait.

I have presented only the most common rigs in this chapter. Anglers are always discovering new and inventive ways to create new rigs or modified versions of existing rigs. This practice is indeed, **fishing different.** The next chapter illustrates one of the new and creative ways to re-purpose old lures.

CHAPTER THIRTEEN

Trying Something Different

"In the end, it's not the years in your life that count. It's the life in your years."

Abraham Lincoln

A few years ago when I decided to write "The Catfish Hunters," I was 75 years old and I felt I needed a younger opinion in that book, so I invited Mac Byrum to co-author the book with me. Mac was a young 73 at the time but I felt that he had forgotten more about the subject than I ever knew. We worked, traveled, and fished together researching the book and became even better friends than we were when we started. We have maintained that friendship ever since.

On many occasions during the preparation of that book, we discussed some of the issues related to catfishing. Among those issues was the idea that catfish anglers seemed to be a special breed. In general, they only like to fish for catfish.

On the other hand, many every-day anglers don't want to fish for catfish, they just don't understand the challenge or the excitement of catching monster fish. We talked a lot about this situation but never really did anything about it.

On a sunny May afternoon, Mac and I were sitting on his porch overlooking Lake Norman. I was talking about my theory on cavitation as it related to the detection capability of fish and also my theory about the creation of "dentrails" that are caused by cavitation voids that are detectable by fish finding Sonar. Mac wasn't saying much about my theory, but I eventually realized that he had really been thinking about what I was saying.

"Do you think that top water lures like the Xrap and the Devil Horse create a cavitation effect with their front and rear mounted propellers?" Mac asked. I was somewhat shocked that he had so quickly related my cavitation theory to a top water lure with a propeller. I believed that top water lures created a disturbance on the surface that drew the attention of fish, but I had not thought about the possible cavitation effect if used under water.

"We don't think of catfish as a fish that attacks lures but catfish do have more sensing capability in their bodies than most other fish so they should be able to detect a spinning propeller on a lure" Mac quickly responded. "If we could drag a top water lure with propellers down near the bottom, we should be able to not only attract fish that are holding deep but it should also be attractive to catfish. This would provide a rig that had catch-all capability. It would be attractive to catfish and all other species that are hanging around in the deeper water. This would introduce all anglers many different species. Anglers who like to catch 2 pound bass might get interested if they caught a 20 pound catfish."

It was getting late in the afternoon and we parted thinking about this new concept in rigging.

Mac apparently couldn't let the thought pass and as soon as I left he went to his garage and dug out a couple of old Devil Horse lures and put together this new "catch all" rig. A few days later he called me all excited and invited me to fish with him the next morning to test the new rig. Knowing Mac, he had already used the rig and wanted me to be a witness to its success.

Early the next morning we were on the lake doing a slow troll close to shore using the new "catch all" lures. The area we were fishing was an area that had serious variations in the bottom contour with depths ranging from three feet to thirty feet. Within two minutes of setting the rods out, I got my first fish, a nice 12 inch crappie. Even before I had that crappie back into the water I got another nice crappie on another rod.

As we passed through an area of 25 foot deep water, I hooked a nice spotted bass about two pounds. Not more than thirty minutes later I caught three catfish, one small flathead, a 5 pound blue cat and a small channel catfish. All of these fish were caught on the new "catch all" rig within a one hour of leaving Mac's dock.

I was now sold on this "catch all" concept. As we fished I was thinking about some minor changes that we might make to the rig but they were truly minor. The basic elements of this new rig are shown below

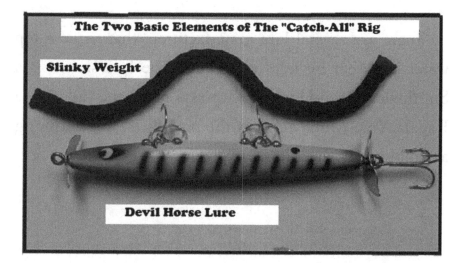

The Two Basic Elements of The "Catch-All" Rig

Slinky Weight

Devil Horse Lure

The slinky weight is growing in popularity as a weight used for dragging along the bottom. It is made from parachute rope which has a hollow center that can be stuffed with small lead weights. The weight can be controlled by the length of the rope used and of course the number of lead shots used. The weight of the lure is ⅜ ounce so it is important that the slinky be at least ¾ to one ounce to keep the weight on the bottom. The top water lure will have the constant tendency to pull up on the weight and we consider it important that the slinky always be dancing along the bottom. That bottom movement might give the rig the effect of a crawfish rapidly moving across the bottom. One advantage of using slinky's is that they very rarely hook up on bottom debris as other large weights often do. Anglers can make their own slinky's or they can be purchased from some sporting goods stores.

There are several lure manufacturers that make a top water lure that includes propellers. The lure shown is a Smithwick Devil Horse. I have also made the rig using a Rapala Xrap which also has the propellers. The entire rig assembly is shown below.

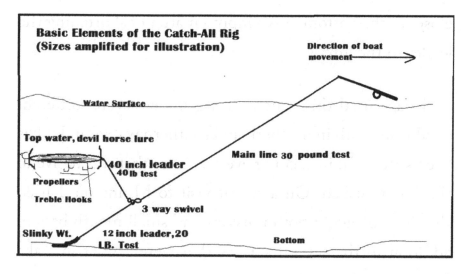

Because of the variety of fish that are caught on this rig, it is suggested that the angler use a medium action casting combination with a line test of at least 30 pounds.

A three way swivel is used to attach both the weight leader and the lure leader. The leader to the lure from the three-way should be about 40 inches so that when trolled, the lure will be slightly above that distance from the bottom. The leader to the slinky weight should be of a 20 pound test and about 12 inches long. The reasoning with these line tests is that if the slinky actually does get hung on some bottom structure, its leader with break before either of the other two lines. If the hook up cannot be released, the only element lost will be the slinky and not the more expensive lure. If the angler prefers to fish closer to the bottom, it is simply a matter of shortening the leader to the lure.

I have used this "catch all' rig under several different conditions both in northern and southern waters and it has been successful in caching every species that was native to the waters fished. On a recent visit to Minnesota I used the rig and caught both muskies and small mouth bass in addition to the several species that were caught in Lake Norman in the south.

I have had a few situations where the slinky was hooked up and lost but these occasions are rare. I am considering a modification to the slinky by putting a small piece of shrink wrap tape over the front end of the weight to eliminate the two small sharp corners. This should help avoid future slinky hook-ups and losses.

This new catch-all rig is an excellent example of how a young mind housed in an old body can help you with your efforts to go **Fishing Different.**

CHAPTER FOURTEEN

Some Less Significant Angling Ideas

"Great minds discuss ideas. Average minds discuss events.
Small minds discuss people."

Eleanor Roosevelt

The Issue of Live Bait Species

Using live bait to catch game fish is not a subject that you can discuss with any professional angler because in their competitive world it is outlawed. But this book was not written specifically for those professionals because they have already gained so much experience they have their theories carved in stone. But for those of us who simply enjoy the sport, the use of live bait is not uncommon. As a matter of fact, it has become quite common for the part time angler.

I have participated in many conversations with experienced part time anglers who have carved their own theory in stone about the best species of bait fish to use and these people stick strongly to their beliefs. Of course there are a few standards that we can use when selecting the best bait. The first and most important standard is to use live bait that is a normal resident of the waters being fished. Not only is this common sense, but in many cases it is also the law. Most states have laws that do not permit an angler to use any live bait that is not already in the waters they fish. These rules have been made to prevent the introduction of new species into waters that already have resident species.

In many lakes there are a variety of species of bait fish in residence such as shiners, threadfin shad and gizzard shad. In these cases an angler often has a dilemma as to which species of bait fish will produce the best results and this is where those "carved in stone" theories come into play.

I happen to be a guy that finds it easier to use shiners simply because they are readily available for sale in local fishing stores. Some anglers that fish the same waters will swear that gizzard shad catch more fish in these waters than shiners. Others feel that the threadfin shad are best. Those who believe the shad concept spend considerable time trying to catch their favorite species using whatever technique is available to them or they travel considerable distances to purchase their favorite species.

At one point a couple of years ago I decided to test my theory about bait fish species. My theory is that it really makes no difference. Predator game fish have several sensing capabilities, among them being the sense of smell, vibration, taste, and sight. Since most game fish are eating all of the time, they are nearly always on the hunt for food. The senses of smell, taste, or vibration might point them in the direction of that food, but before they attack it they must first see it. So I believe the most important sense in this case is the sense of sight.

The eyesight of fish is not similar to the eyesight of humans. Different fish species have different capabilities to recognize colors as an example. So what would make a predator fish attack one species of bait fish over another species?

I decided to further investigate what different species of bait fish would look like under water so I purchased six fish of four different species that were available in my region. I put all of these fish into my bait tank with fresh new clear water. After a period of time to let the fish settle and mingle, I dropped my underwater camera into the tank and carefully studied and photographed the video screen of the images that I saw. Once of the many images is shown below.

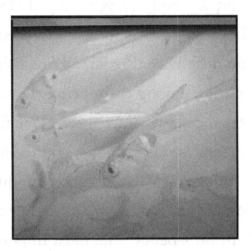

What I am showing here is a photo of a video screen so the definition could be much better, but the main point here is that the only thing that is immediately visible on all of the fish, no matter their species, is their eyes, and to a lesser extend the spot on the side of the shad. To my eye, none of these fish looked any more attractive as a meal than any other of them. The thing that is most dominant to the naked eye is the eye of each fish. I believe that it is the eye of the bait fish that becomes the center of the target of the predator.

Some will argue that shad send out a different smell because they are oilier than a shiner. That oily smell would make them more attractive to the predator. I believe that once a predator spots the eye it is game over regardless of the bait fish species.

I feel so strongly about my theory that I went to by favorite big box fishing supply store and purchased hundreds of artificial stick-on eyes. I examined every lure that I owned and I immediately stuck an artificial eye on any that had no eyes.

I have never run any good tests to determine if lures with eyes catch more fish than those with no eyes because I no longer have any lures with no eyes. I do believe fairly strongly, however, that my eye theory is correct.

I also use as a very shaky support of my theory about the eyes the fact that predators nearly always want to eat their food so the bait fish enters their throat head first to avoid the damage caused by the spines on their dorsal fin. Having the eye as a target helps position the bait for the predators' attack. I admit that this part of my theory is weak, but it does make as much sense as some of the other fishing myths I have heard.

Increasing Your Angling Excitement with Photos

There probably is no angler alive today who has not been in possession of a photo showing the catch just made. My family calls these photos "man holding fish" and these photos are the subject of some humor among non-anglers. Websites, blogs, books, and magazine articles all include photos of smiling anglers holding or standing by their catches. This has become part of our fishing tradition. But! I feel for the most part the photos are being taken for granted and may possibly be causing some harm to the fish when the angler takes too much time preparing for the proud photo, causing the fish to become starved of critical oxygen.

I recently discovered a better use of photography that has added excitement to my angling experiences – underwater photos of the fish. I received an underwater camera system several years ago that included a submersible camera attached by cable to a video screen. As hard as I tried, I could never make this system work. The camera was only effective if it was kept absolutely still and I couldn't find a way to attract the fish toward the eye of the camera.

Two years ago I received a Go Pro camera system and my photo experiences changed radically and added a good deal of excitement to my fishing experiences. However, my first problem was to find a way to get the camera deep enough in the water to photograph the fish.

I had retired my golf clubs a year earlier but I remembered that I had a ball retriever in the bag. This retriever was an aluminum pole that could be extended to about six feet. I quickly grabbed this retriever, cut off the cup at the tip, and screwed on the camera adapter that came with the Go Pro camera. Now my underwater system was ready for action, all I needed was some fairly clear water. The first few photos I took of fish I was retrieving only provided good practice, the water clarity was not good and I needed a great deal of practice with the multi-tasking required to retrieve a fish with the rod in one hand and the camera holder in the other hand. This was possible, but not very effective.

I soon realized that to get good pictures of fish required two people working together: one retrieving the fish and the other operating the camera. Early last year I was fishing in Clear Lake in Canada and the lake lived up to its name. The water was crystal clear and the potential for great underwater photos was at hand.

I had two objectives for this trip. I wanted to catch a five pound smallmouth bass and I wanted to get some good photos of the fish habitat underwater. I accomplished both goals.

The first photo I took was a northern pike, hooked by a fishing lure, fighting close to the bottom. This photo is shown below.

This photo showed not only the fish but showed splendid images of the bottom growth and rocks. This was not a monster pike, only about 24 inches but it displayed great photographic characteristics.

Later in the day I hooked a hard fighting smallmouth bass which I later realized was the five pound plus fish I was after. Not only did I get the fish, but also a great photo of the fighting bass shown below.

The trip provided many other great photos and the quality of the photos increased as my fishing partner and I got more experience working together when fish were being retrieved. The biggest problem was mental. When big fish were on the line, the angler was anxious to get the fish into the boat and off the line and patience often prevented providing enough time to properly photograph the fish. It only took a couple of looks at the photos to overcome this impatience. We both realized that the quality of the photos was greatly improved if the angler operating the rod simply took his time with the retrieve and played to the direction of the producer operating the camera.

The big gain of this photographing experience was the increase in activity and excitement of viewing a great photo of the fish in its natural environment. I also believe that this photographic technique helps insure the health of the fish. They spend much less time out of the water and in most cases they were released without having to bring the fish out of the water at all.

I am currently exploring additional techniques for operating the camera and retrieving the fish myself without any help. I have mounted a fixture to the handle of my net but I have not yet perfected that technique. Adding the GoPro to your angling experiences is a real example of **Fishing Different.**

CHAPTER FIFTEEN

To Sleep or Not to Sleep, That is the Question

"Tell me and I forget. Teach me and I remember. Involve me and I learn."

Benjamin Franklin

One of the meaningful unsolved questions about fish behavior relates to whether or not fish have periods of sleep and, if so, when these periods occur. There are many subjects where an interested angler can, with persistence, study and answer behavioral questions regarding fish activities. Some of these investigations have resulted in significant changes in angling practices over the years. Others have created myths that have simply been accepted, and in some cases, are now being challenged, as I do in my books. This question, however, does not lend itself to being answered by the average angler, but may be answered by interested scientists and biologists. Even their task will be substantial because observing fish in their natural environment on a repeated basis is extremely difficult.

Most documented information on this subject has resulted from fish that were confined to an observation tank. These results, although valuable, are probably not applicable to fish resident in natural water bodies because observation tanks lack the element of survival and predatory behavior.

Since I have taken a rather firm position on the subject of the best times of the day for fishing, and I presented this opinion elsewhere in this book, the subject of the sleeping habits of fish is very important to support my conclusions on thIS subject. Therefore, I have attempted to dig deeper into available research and to apply some practical scientific logic to that information.

I have always found it useful to compare fish behavior to the behavior of humans. In the first stage of my studies I wanted to try to get an acceptable definition of sleep as we humans understand it. Putting aside the medical journals' definition of sleep, it is fairly uniformly agreed that sleep for most humans and mammals involves the closure of eyelids and a specific slowing of the brainwave pattern in the neocortex of the brain. This makes it fairly easy for researchers to determine when a person, another mammal, or bird is sleeping. This creates a problem for me since fish have no eyelids and the brain of a fish has no neocortex so the definition of sleep for fish cannot be compared to that of humans and other animals.

Researchers have generally re-defined sleep for fish as being comprised of: inactivity for extended periods of time; a resting posture; routine behavior; and a reduced sensitivity to the surrounding environment. None of these criteria, however, have been absolutely defined. I am mostly concerned with the last criteria because I believe that Nature has given fish an extraordinary capability to sense danger or any threat to its survival.

Observations, again in a captive environment, have shown that some fish seem to take short rests by resting on the bottom in small surface irregularities. Some bullheads (catfish) have been observed with their fins and tail positioned in such a fashion to permit them to settle into a ten degree angle rest along the bottom. It is reported that bass and some species of perch were observed resting on or under logs or other bottom structure. Some fish like mackerel and bluefish, never seem to rest, swimming constantly. The swimming pattern of these two species does, however, slow down at night.

All credible scientific studies have shown that when fish are in their resting positions, their cardiac and respiratory rates have decreased as did the movement of their mouth, gills, and eyes. Even a sleeping fish would require some heart and lung function since fish absorb their oxygen by passing water through their gills. Since nearly every study I have investigated has concluded that many but not all species of fish do take rest periods, there appears to be no evidence that these rest periods are actually sleep as it has been biologically defined. There has also been little or no indication when these rest periods actually take place during a normal 24 hour day.

One credible study put forth the view that sleep for an animal serves as a great immobilizer, forcing animals to stay quiet, avoid detection by predators, and save energy during unprofitable periods of a 24 hour cycle. I can take a great deal from this theory as it applies to fish based upon past studies I have done and published in previous books.

The critical part of my research on related subjects involves the subject of the neocortex of a brain. It is well studied and medically known that the neocortex of a human brain is the area of the brain that serves as the "central computer" of the nervous system. The thousands of nerve endings in the human body are the sensors that pick up external forces that act on the body. As an example, if we touch a hot surface with our fingers, the nerve endings in our fingers send a signal to the neocortex of the brain. That processor tells the brain that what is being felt is pain from the excessive heat. The finger tip sensors do not know it is pain until told that by the brain. The brain's neocortex also permits the brain to store that information in its memory for future reference.

Scientists have proven that the brain of a fish is very small in size compared to the relative size of a human brain and therefore cannot contain all of the capability of the human brain. Because of this small size, many of the functions that the human brain possesses are absent in the brain of a fish. The most significant of these missing elements is the neocortex.

There have been widespread arguments throughout the research community about the ability of a fish to feel pain. The basic science of these arguments is very clear: without the neocortex in the brain to process the pain sensation, no pain as we understand it is felt by a fish. If a significant trauma is applied to the body of a fish, like dropping it on to a hard surface, or handling a retrieve in a prolonged manner, this trauma, if repeated can result in the fish developing a trauma memory.

There are many examples of how this trauma memory has been used to our advantage. When NASA first conducted its studies of the behavior of humans in space, it used chimpanzees as study objects. They found that by repeated reward and punishment, these animals would eventually learn behavioral changes by command. Many other animals like dogs and horses are being trained using the same trauma techniques that were developed decades ago.

Since a fish has no neocortex, it cannot develop a memory the way humans think of it and therefore the brain of a fish must use other sensing capability to alter its behavior in a manner that would look to us like sleep.

We know that the metabolism variations in the body of a fish change its behavior with significant changes in water temperature. This is a capability that nature provides fish that slows down the overall functions of its body when the water temperature gets overly hot or cold. This actually slows down the body functions, reduces the need for the intake of food and causes periods of extended reduced activity. Extreme cold or extreme hot water is detected by the metabolism system as trauma to the fish and it automatically responds by forcing behavioral changes to the fish. Here again, the hot or cold water can be considered a trauma to the fish, against which it must react.

Exertion is also a trauma that deserves a reaction. On several occasions I have observed large fish, such as northern pike and muskies, putting up a tremendous fight and causing a prolonged retrieve while being caught that literally wears out the fish. At the end of the fight the fish is so exhausted it often cannot use its natural abilities to regain stability or even swim in its normal fashion. When this happens, experienced anglers know how to help revive the fish by holding it by the tail and causing forward and backward movement so that oxygen can again be created by movement of water through the gill plates. I believe this type trauma caused by a hard retrieve is remembered by the fish and will cause it to rest for a long period of time, perhaps days, before it attempts to eat again.

I have personally observed many cases where a large school of perch seem to hold in one spot for a prolonged period of time, permitting an angler to sit on top of the school and catch great numbers of fish. On other occasions I have also observed similar schools of perch that are on the move and rarely stop to rest. Having studied these movements of perch schools I have concluded that the perch schools which are generally on the move, do require a period of rest at least once during a 24 hour period.

Earlier in this book I explained the functioning of the lateral line in a fish. This amazing system provides fish the "virtual" capability to detect other moving objects far out beyond their individual strike zone. The lateral line system has the detection and warning capability to alert a fish that danger may be imminent or a food source is near. The lateral line is the advanced alert radar system for every fish. There is no indication that the lateral line system ever slows down or malfunctions unless it is damaged by extreme handling by an angler.

It is my opinion that the combination of the metabolic system and the lateral line system are the trauma detecting systems that tell a fish when it must rest. Yes, fish can get tired but that tiredness is caused by excessive trauma. Under normal non-threatening conditions, the swim bladder of a fish permits it to remain still in the water without using its tail or fins for stabilization. In a non-current condition, most fish can remain at rest whenever they wish. If conditions arise, as they often do, where a fish is required to swim rapidly to avoid a predator, or rough water requires continuous movement or perhaps a situation exists where a feeding frenzy is created, I believe a fish takes what we define as a "power nap." These power naps replace the sleep periods that other humans, mammals, and animals require.

Sleep deprivation studies have shown that fish deprived of these power naps for extended periods of time will eventually make up for this loss by taking longer naps when time permits. These periods of "catch-up" permit the fish to regain the energy lost by previous traumatic experiences.

There are several situations that are shown to be sleepless periods for fish or periods when they have no rest at all. These occasions include the following:

1. **Migration** periods when fish are moving from one area to another over a long distance. Salmon moving upstream to breed would be one of these situations.

2. **Spawning** periods are day and night periods and usually keep fish alert at all times.

3. **Post** spawn periods where the males or females are guarding the eggs deposited in the nests. The eggs require oxygen and the fanning of the nest is thought to provide the needed oxygen.

What is the Best Time For a Nap?

There is very little published material that discusses the sleep time frame best suited for most fish. This might be the time to apply some practical logic to the subject. I have made the very strong point earlier in this book that the greatest enemy to all fish is the availability of sunshine. Fish have no eyelids so they will always shy away from sunlight.

Every fish is conditioned by Nature to be aware of all threats against its survival. Generally a fish has to be seen to be attacked and for most fish sight is reduced during the hours of darkness.

It is generally agreed that the hours shortly after sunrise and shortly before sunset are good times to fish because the predator fish are aware that smaller fish are either going to or returning from their feeding spots. Why would any fish nap during these exciting times.

Heavy angling activity causes situations where all underwater life is subject to changes in conditions. The presence of moving lures, active bait fish, and moving boats are periods of alert for game fish. Their senses would tell them to remain alert during these times of heavy fishing activity.

To me, this would force the conclusion that if a fish is going to rest or take a power nap, it will do it during the hours of darkness when the threat is at a minimum. There might be an exception for some species like walleyes that are sometimes more active during hours of darkness.

What can we conclude from all of this? Are we still in the position of saying we really don't know? I don't think so. I believe we can conclude with the application of some logic that fish do not sleep as we understand sleeping but they do take short periods of rest or "power naps" and most of these naps are taken during the hours of reduced light. The need for the power naps is brought about by the daily trauma of fish life, chasing and being chased tires or traumatizes the fish and this trauma dictates rest periods or naps. We should understand however, that the over-riding instinct for survival will cause the lateral line system to warn or awaken a fish if a natural or artificial food source is approaching. So! Do not let the resting habits of game fish cause you to **Fish Different**. If you suspect that you are seeking resting or napping fish, no matter what time of the day or night, simply add an extra cast or two or make an additional pass with your troll to assure that you get the attention of the fish after it regains its alertness.

CHAPTER SIXTEEN

GPS Confusion Among Anglers

"It has become appallingly obvious that our technology has exceeded our humanity."

Albert Einstein

It was March 22, 2003 and millions of Americans were watching their TV screens as our aircraft were making a precision assault on Bagdad Iraq. Close-up pictures flashed across the screen as bombs delivered from aircraft flying miles away flew right down the chimneys of selected targets and demolished buildings suspected of housing key enemy forces. Most of us were amazed at the precision accuracy of these weapons.

Not too many weeks after those TV videos, I was doing a fishing lecture and talking about how fish finding sonar equipment that included GPS capability was revolutionizing the fishing world. I was interrupted in my lecture by a fairly experienced angler who asked, "We can put bombs into chimneys from five miles away delivered from aircraft traveling at five hundred miles per hour and I can't find the rock pile that the State recently put into our lake." Several other attendees at the lecture joined in the mild revolt indicating that the GPS coordinates that were published by the State did not put them on the rock piles, "we simply can't find the rock piles using the information published."

I indicated that I would look into the problem and talk about the situation at the next lecture. After the meeting I asked for the coordinates that were being used and I immediately realized what was wrong. The published coordinates were map coordinates and not GPS coordinates. Generally this would not make a difference if a boater wanted to find the general area, but map coordinates are often not exactly like GPS coordinates.

There are three ways that coordinates can be given. The most popular method is to list the coordinates as degrees, minutes and seconds. This might list a location as N35 31 7.4, W80 56 20.3. The west coordinates would read 80 degrees, 56 minutes, 20.3 seconds. Seems like a very detailed coordinate except that it is not in the form accepted by most GPS receiving equipment. Map coordinates are usually shown in degrees, minutes and seconds as shown above. The second method defines the coordinates in degrees and decimal degrees. This would show the above coordinates as N35.51872, W 80.93898. We normally do not see this method used but it is also correct but not accepted by GPS receivers.

The method accepted by most GPS receivers uses degrees and decimal minutes. This would produce the above position as N35 31.124, W80 56.339. These are the coordinates that will be accepted by your GPS receiver.

This part of the problem is fairly well known and there are several conversion programs available in the internet that will make the necessary calculations. All that is necessary is to search "GPS conversion charts" and select any of the programs that are provided.

Having provided this information at my next lecture, I began to get e-mails indicating that the anglers still could not find the rock piles with the conversion data I provided. Now confused, I decided to do a little more research about the GPS system.

My first and simplest action was to take my boat out and see if I had the same problem. Indeed I did. Reaching the precise GPS coordinates I had, the rock pile was not there. I circled and searched and finally found the target but it was nearly 200 feet from the published coordinates. This now warranted some detailed investigation of the system itself to see if there was some inherent systemic problem causing the inaccuracies.

I was not unfamiliar with the early Government desire to develop the system. I was working in the aerospace industry in the early 1970's when the Defense Department issued a request for proposal to all of its suppliers. I was assigned to the design team preparing my company's proposal. Our design team worked very hard for many months to try to satisfy the Government's performance requirements. After many long and grueling technical arguments, we finally concluded that a system such as this could not be designed to the performance requirements that demanded and we withdrew from the competition. We were apparently very wrong because the first GPS satellite was launched in 1975. It's performance was very different from the original stated requirements but it was a start. After many design changes the last of a system of 24 satellites was launched in June of 1993, nearly 20 years after the first launch.

The entire GPS system now consists of 32 satellites, 24 of which are in system operation at all times. Each satellite carries up to four atomic clocks which are periodically updated by a ground station. The satellites transmit precise timing signals and position data. A GPS receiver decodes the timing signals from several of the satellites, interpreting the arrival times and latitude, longitude, and altitude with an uncertainty as large as 10 meters. This uncertainty started to interest me and I continued to dig for more information.

The 24 GPS satellites orbit at four slightly different levels at about 12,600 miles above the earth. Each satellite orbits the earth twice each day transmitting with a power level of only 30 watts. The satellites operate off of solar power but have back-up batteries in case of some solar system anomaly.

The Government admits to a system accuracy goal of 15 meters 95% of the time. Some experts have admitted that at times the system errors accumulate to nearly 30 meters. This could result in a system error from the satellites of more than 90 feet.

This level of error began to interest me and I started to look into the accuracy of the GPS equipment most of us are using on our boats. Published information from one reputable supplier indicated that their receiver accuracy varies between 10 and 30 meters with an average accuracy of 15 meters. This means that at any time your receiver equipment can be as far off as 30 meters which equates to more than 90 feet. Add this to the 90 foot error possible from the GPS system and your receiver error could read as far off the target as 180 feet.

OH! There is more. I recently took a photo of my old GPS equipment as I was reading a GPS location. That photo is shown below.

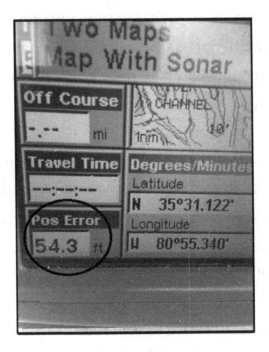

Notice the little box in the lower left indicating my system error at that time was 54.3 feet. I'm not sure if this adds to the above error but consider this.

When the rock piles were placed in the lake, their GPS positions were measured by equipment just like mine. As a matter of fact, when the State put more than 300 fish attractors in the lake over a three year period, I actually took many of the locations with my equipment. That means that the published coordinates themselves had an initial error of more than 54 feet. Add this to the possible 180 foot error of the GPS system and it now appears possible that we could have a total error of more than 230 feet on any single GPS location.

So anglers, don't get frustrated when you search for the rock piles or fish attractors in your waters, you just might have to circle around to compensate for this possible 230 foot error of the system. When you do finally locate the target, it will appear on your sonar similar to one of the two images shown below.

I personally visited two of the recently built rock piles in Lake Norman 5 days after they were built and I found many large bass congregating near them. This proves the effectiveness of these structures toward attracting game fish. It might take a little detection work to find the targets but once located you will have great success **Fishing Different.**

CHAPTER SEVENTEEN

The Latest Craze – Ultraviolet Light

"A lie gets halfway around the world before the truth has a chance to get its pants on."

Sir Winston Churchill

When I previously described some of the work of the real inventors in our society like Torricelli or Berti or Pascal, these men achieved their fame only after many grueling hours or even years of tests to prove their theories. In some notable cases they even consulted with each other to insure that their work carried with it the corroboration of the world's leading minds.

Even Einstein took years of study by other scientists to validate his theory of relativity by traveling the globe following solar eclipse events to measure the relative movement of other terrestrial bodies.

Today, there seems to be more a tendency to throw an idea out there and see if it takes hold. If it does it usually becomes a fad or even a myth, like some of the theories I have discussed previously in this book. Some of these myths last for years and some die early deaths.

Fishing is not without its share of these so called theories and one of those theories involves the ability of fish to see ultraviolet light. Lure manufacturers have grabbed on to this idea, and without any credible testing or even knowledgeable input, they have loaded the shelves of sporting goods stores with ultraviolet lures and ultraviolet paints that promise to catch more fish than anything previously known to mankind. Unfortunately, anglers are buying into the concept and loading their tackle boxes with new and apparently more visible lures. It only takes one professional winning one tournament to brag about his new ultra-visible lure and anglers rush out to buy as many as they can afford. The theory of the believers is that ultraviolet light makes everything look brighter and if it's brighter it will attract more fish.

It's a little too early in this new craze for me to make a conclusive statement about the validity of this concept, but when it comes to the science of the idea, I am a doubter.

When I was writing my book "The Catfish Hunters," I did some research on the eyesight of different fish species because many experienced anglers believed that catfish have very bad eyesight. I also determined at the time there was considerable conflicting opinion on the subject. The core of that argument was the ability of a catfish to see colors.

The anatomy of the human eye and the eye of most fish are similar in many respects. Both have a cornea, an iris, a pupil, a lens, and a retina. The process of turning light into an image starts at the retina, the parabolic shaped surface at the rear of the eye. Photons of light are received and transformed into electrical impulses that are then sent to the brain. The retina contains photosensitive receptors which are called rods and cones. The rods and cones accomplish the task of collecting the light entering the eye and transforming it into impulses and directing it through nerve fibers to the brain.

The major difference between the human eye and the eye of a fish is the light passing through the air toward the human eye is passing through a much less dense media than when passing through water. Because air and the human cornea have different densities, the light entering the human cornea is bent to enter the pupil. Water and the cornea are close to the same density so light entering the eye of a fish does not witness density change and is not bent to enter the pupil.

For humans, the iris is the colored aperture that opens and closes depending on the intensity of the light that is entering the eye. In fish, the iris is fixed, making the pupil a fixed size. For a fish to adjust its eyes to a changing intensity of light, the retina adjusts the position of the photoreceptors, the rods and the cones. For humans, this adjustment takes seconds but for fish is can take several minutes to make that same adjustment. This adjustment period in fish is much longer for very small fish than it is for larger predator fish. Some biologists have reasoned that this time difference between large and small fish is the main reason why predator fish feed mostly during periods of sunrise and sunset because predator fish can adjust to the light change faster than their prey.

Fish that live at significantly different depths have different numbers of rods and cones. Rods control the amount of light that enters the eye and cones control the amount of color that enters. Fish that live very deep in the water have many more rods than cones since color essentially disappears in deep water. Fish that live mostly in shallow water have nearly equal numbers of rods and cones.

Ultraviolet light makes up a portion of the electromagnetic spectrum, with wavelengths just slightly shorter than those of the visible light spectrum. Humans cannot see ultraviolet light as a specific color because we do not have a dedicated photoceptor or cone in our retina that is sensitive to ultraviolet light.

According to Dr. Ellis Loew, a professor at Cornell University, some very small fish have an ultraviolet receptor when born but they lose it as they grow. Most of the predator fish that anglers seek cannot see ultraviolet light as adults because they do not have the correct receptors.

Dr. Loew indicates that when humans see so called ultraviolet lures exposed to black light, they are not really seeing the ultraviolet light but they are really seeing reflected brighteners that coat the lures and cause it to fluoresce. Fluorescence makes the light brighter but the lure does not become self illuminating.

The ability to observe this brightening is very dependent on the ability of the additive to penetrate the water. In stained water this penetration will be only a foot or so, possibly two feet. Beyond that depth there would be little or no brightening effect. In exceptionally clear water, penetration might reach as deep as 100 feet and would possibly have an effect. The question here however is how many anglers fish in clear water that deep. Probably not many.

I suppose I could speculate that at some point in the future a lure manufacturer will build a lure with a black light attached to create visible brightness but until that time I will remain hesitant to buy any ultraviolet lures to significantly improve my catch rate. The science just does not justify it.

CHAPTER EIGHTEEN

Cross-over, Fresh Water to Salt Water

"Twenty years from now you will be more disappointed by the things that you didn't do than by the ones you did. So throw off the bowline. Catch the trade winds in your sails. Explore, Dream, Discover."

Mark Twain

For most anglers, fishing in fresh or salt water is usually a matter of where they live. Those who live within easy access to the ocean have probably developed techniques that favor salt water fishing. Those who live a considerable distance inland normally favor fresh water angling. I have had occasion over the course of my life to live in both regions but since I was raised on fresh water fishing, I never really felt that ocean fishing offered me the same challenges that I derived from catching freshwater fish. On average, ocean fish tend to be larger and one would think that size would make me favor that environment, but it didn't. I always believed that the joy of fishing was the thrill of using light gear and feeling the entire experience as the fish fought the inevitable retrieve.

A few years ago I started to change that feeling when I was introduced to fishing for red drum in the shallow waters of the southeastern shore in Lake Charles, Louisiana.

Red drum are sometimes called channel bass, redfish, spottail bass or simply reds. They are found in the Atlantic Ocean from Massachusetts to Florida and in the Gulf of Mexico from Florida all the way to Northern Mexico. They are a pinkish-red color on their back which fades to a white color on the belly. Red drum have eyespots near their tail and some of the older fish have multiple spots. A three year old red drum usually weighs around six to eight pounds. Those that grow to over twenty seven inches are called "bull reds". They tend to hang out in seagrass in shallow water and they like muddy and sandy bottom areas. They are often found near oyster bars. Some scientists feel that nature provided the spots near the tail of the fish to mislead any attackers into thinking that the tail is really the head of the fish, making it easier for the reds to escape capture by larger predators.

My first experience fishing for reds surprised me in that the gear used was exactly like that which I often used for fresh water fish. The gear consisted of medium weight rods and matched spinning reels. Since we were fishing for large fish, the line was braid, testing at about 20 pounds. The hook in this instance was a jay hook, tipped with small shrimp. I was taken to an area where an oyster bed was about three feet below the surface. It didn't take long before I landed my first big red. I was used to the fight of a fresh water striper that always took the bait down and sideways once hooked. In this shallow water the fish could not go deeper but it made up for that by constantly moving sideways, offering a challenge that exceeded that of a striper. I was pleased with this nice 10 pound red shown below.

In about three hours I managed to land ten more fish but most of them exceeded the established slot limit and had to be released, as did this first fish.

Now I was hooked on fishing for this new species. The fight exceeded any freshwater fish and the use of fresh water gear made me feel at home.

My enthusiasm quickly made me investigate another red fishing experience, this time at Hatteras, North Carolina. Again the reds were located in the grass fields north of Ocracoke Island in the Pamlico Sound. Here the gear was the same, medium spinning gear, but now we were using simple gold weedless spoons similar to those that I had used many times to cast for northern pike in Canada. Here, that boat captain was standing high above the water on his perch attempting to sight the schools of reds. Once he spotted the fish he simply told us the direction to cast and the line was quickly stiff with a nice fish. In North Carolina the limit on reds is one per angler and we easily kept our limit on that trip.

Most recently I decided to try South Carolina reds in Georgetown, SC. My friend Rich Doering and I fished with Captain Fred Rourk and we had another great day. Unfortunately all of the reds that we caught were too large to keep but they were great for photos.

Now I consider myself totally hooked on fishing for these salt water reds. I have been told that the real big fish are located close to the Mississippi River delta near the Texas border. I have now added that trip to my bucket list.

This cross-over from fresh to salt water fishing for me is a real example of **Fishing Different.** I can use all of my freshwater skills and equipment to catch really big fish averaging ten to twenty pounds each and are a very good eating fish.

CHAPTER NINETEEN

Your Fishing Style Will Govern Your Angling Success

"Perfection is not attainable, but if we chase perfection we can catch excellence."

Vince Lombardi

When I selected **Fishing Different** as the title of this book, I did that because my experience has shown me that most anglers, including beginners and experienced individuals, want to learn how to adopt the successful techniques of other anglers to improve their catch rate. I have also learned that most anglers, except first timers, have already developed a style or technique that they are comfortable with. In some cases it is due to the areas in which they live and their access to local waters. In other instances it is the fishing habits of their teachers, usually a parent or friend. Others may have learned from television shows where catching fish is often made to look very easy.

Anglers who live in or near the mountains have probably chosen stream fishing with fly fishing equipment as their primary interest. Those who live near or have access to a farm pond have learned the techniques for success in that environment. The many rivers that weave their way throughout the country have provided waters that demand a different style. Lakes usually result in fishing from a boat, which offer many different style options. The oceans, of course, offer the greatest access to big water for those who live comfortable distances from them.

Each of these situations demands a different angling style and in some cases different equipment. It would be impossible for me to provide a book that offers advice to anglers for every one of these situations.

There are, however, common threads that weave their way through every one of these fishing conditions: the behavior of fish being sought; the conditions of the waters; the environment of the surroundings; and the weather. Understanding these common threads will help every angler, no matter where their interests lie, to a better understanding of the steps necessary to improve their angling success.

I have always believed an understanding of the basic science of the common threads of angling will broaden the capability of every angler and eventually increase catch rates no matter which condition or fishing style has been chosen.

I have adopted a strategy in my own life that learning is not an age-related exercise and learning new things every day, no matter what your age, is a fine objective for all of us to have in our lives. Throughout this book I have provided several examples of how I have been forced to abandon many of the long standing myths about fishing I learned as a youngster. In some cases it was difficult for me to accept the new concepts until I took the approach of studying my own data and fishing results that proved many of the old methods were wrong or at lease wrong for my specific fishing circumstances.

I spend a great deal of time teaching others about fishing techniques. I am always quick to remind my students that these are techniques that have been successful for me, and may not be comfortable for them. I always take care to remind my students that others have been successful using angling techniques that are quite different from mine. That's the nice thing about fishing – there is not only one procedure or technique or bait which will succeed. This is why I lean toward an understanding of the underlying science behind the sport. I believe if we understand the basic science, it will apply to any of the many angling situations we might face.

There are some basic conclusions I hope my readers have taken away from reading this book. The most basic of these conclusions is that you will never catch fish under any circumstances if you don't have your line in the water with bait that appeals to the fish. Improvement of your catch rate will come from continued practice of your selected angling technique. Since 90% of the fish in any water body are located in 10% of the area, your first chore is to study your fishing location in an attempt to locate those areas.

Don't be fooled by some of the popular weather related concepts about fronts, barometric pressure, or the location of the moon. To som, these factors are important. To me they are simply detractors from the simple theory that the position of the sun in the sky and its penetration in the water is the single factor that should govern your fishing technique. Fish can be caught at any time of the day or night if you adopt your technique to that specific condition, and understand how the fish behavior changes with the conditions.

Please don't fall victim to the latest angling fad or lure advertisement. Most of these are simply marketing ploys to lure you toward spending more money for the newest and latest gimmick. Remember, the worm or night crawler has always been and will continue to be the most desired food for nearly every species of fish. If actual worms are not available, then use the best available imitation of the worm that you can find and hook it in a fashion that will produce the greatest movement.

Fish behavior is very predictable. Unless affected by significant natural changes, fish react to changes in water temperature, the changing seasons, location of food, and the penetration of the sun. If you understand these factors you will improve your success rate. Rapid or drastic changes in the weather will cause behavioral changes in the fish. Fishing immediately after a major weather change might cause great frustration for anglers. Wait two or three days after a major storm and fish behavior will return to its normal state.

At this stage of our fishing history, the sonar based fish finders are the most useful technological tool for any angler using a boat on the water. It is extremely important for every angler to understand the basics of this equipment, especially the interpretation of the images that are presented to the angler. Sonar information tells you exactly what is happening under your boat and how the fish are behaving around you. An understanding of these images will give you all the information you need to react to the behavior of the fish. The sonar information will tell you the depth to place your bait, the feeding activities of the fish, the underwater structure that will protect fish, the speed of your boat if trolling, and the location of the underwater food sources that will eventually attract the game fish. Every bit of information provided by these fish finders will help you catch more fish. The more recent units that present information in more detail offer the angler more efficient sources of this valuable information.

With today's state of technological advances in all areas of our society, I am concerned that this technology creep has entered the angling arena in a big way. It may be my advanced age, but I am afraid that some of this technology advance will actually harm our sport. As a catch and release angler, I get most of my enjoyment of my fishing experiences from the strike of the fish and the few seconds or sometimes minutes that it takes me to retrieve the fish. That to me is the sport of fishing and the conservation of the fish population by proper handling and return of the fish to its native waters. If we are not careful, some of the new technological features that are entering the sport might be taking away from the basic challenge and even the excitement of fishing. As anglers we should make sure that we apply these new creations in a manner that adds to our enjoyment and excitement and not simply use new ideas to catch more fish.

To become a complete angler, I believe that we should expand our vision of fishing beyond simply our ability to catch fish. Time spent on or near the water can become a very valuable learning experience, not only the learning that comes with fishing success but also the absorbing of the beauties and mysteries of Nature. As a student of Nature, I have become convinced that we can all learn from our surroundings when enjoying the pleasures of fishing. Nature is creating miracles all around us when we are on the water or pursuing other outdoor activities. Nature has provided all animals the instincts necessary for their survival. Without a classroom, television, or book learning, Nature gives wildlife the inherent ability to recognize its signs, like the weather changes, seasonal variations, temperature considerations, and all of this knowledge is simply built in to the natural surroundings in which the wildlife lives.

A good friend of mine once asked me if I would continue to hunt deer if they carried guns. I responded that I would because it would only increase the odds against me in my pursuit. When I am hunting I am in the natural environment of the deer that I hunt, not in my normal environment. That makes me the underdog in that situation.

When I am fishing, I am also not in my comfort zone, but rather fishing in an environment that is most familiar to the fish I am pursuing. That gives the advantage to the fish, not the angler. Every angler has been is a situation where the fish are surrounding the boat but none are biting. Who has the advantage in this situation, the angler with all of the right gear, or the fish that are avoiding the catch? Fish may have tiny brains and no ability to reason, but they have a distinct advantage over anglers in that they are in their natural environment and taught by nature all of the tricks of survival.

Most adults in America today recognize that the world around them is changing. Many of those changes are good and simply reflect a growth in knowledge, technology, and progress. On the other hand, some of the changes reflect a loss of cultural, behavioral, and even religious values that played such a huge role in the growth of our American heritage.

Those who believe our country still houses the best society in the world also recognize the role the family unit played in the development of this great nation. Schools once taught the basics of reading, writing, and arithmetic, blended together by facts of our history. Social behavior, discipline, work ethic, and the basic values for life itself were handled by the family unit or the church. This combination worked well for hundreds of years. It is not working as well today.

Economic conditions have forced parents to spend a great deal of time at work. Social correctness has loaded our schools with subjects unrelated to the basic subjects they once taught. Technology, as great as it has been, has created a social and communication media where our young people are conversing electronically, rather than using the typical verbal communication technique that requires face-to-face discussions. The entertainment media seems driven by violence, and the decaying world situation presents death and destruction as a new world norm. With all of this, should we be surprised that the youth of today often look at the world as a "me" world and not the "us" world that it used to be.

Even in sports, the aspect of competition has slowly eroded with the concept of participation rather than competition where there are no losers or winners. This has apparently been brought about by a desire to have everyone feel good about themselves. But it has also dampened the desire for self improvement and creativity, as well as competitiveness.

You might ask what all this has to do with fishing? In my mind it is quite simple. If we are going to modify our American social beliefs and behavior, we are going to have to do it through the family unit. Parents and youngsters are going to have to regain the spirit of togetherness in activities where they can participate as a unit, interdependent on each other as part of a working team. Fishing is one of the few outdoor activities that hold promise of a healthy and wholesome sport where parents and youngsters can participate together.

There is no other activity that I can think of that can take an individual or a family into an environment where the most stressful activity might be the sound of a loon, calling out to its mate, or the splash of a jumping fish in an otherwise silent lake. The beauty of freshwater fishing is that it can be enjoyed by an individual, in the solitude of a secluded lake or pond, or it can be a family activity, where everyone can participate, not only in the actual fishing activities but also watching the mysteries of nature unfold before their very eyes. A blue heron walking along the shoreline stalking its next meal, demonstrates the cycle of life where nature provides all of its creatures the means of survival. A female deer slowly and silently walks to the water to drink, stops and looks around before she signals to her two small fawns to follow, again a lesson in survival.

Fishing is also an activity that brings out the human spirit for continued improvement, like runners, who always wants to improve their personal best times, anglers always want to catch a fish bigger than their last catch. This eventually develops into the desire to compete with one's self or others and fosters an attitude of competitive self improvement. This improvement comes by learning new techniques and procedures and finding new ways of **Fishing Different.**

Printed in the United States
Bookmasters

Printed in the United States
By Bookmasters